NOT OFF LIMITS

Questions You Wish
You Could Ask at Church

ROSS COCHRAN

LEAFWOOD
PUBLISHERS
an imprint of Abilene Christian University Press

NOT OFF LIMITS
Questions You Wish You Could Ask at Church

P U B L I S H E R S

an imprint of Abilene Christian University Press

Copyright 2014 by Ross Cochran

ISBN 978-0-89112-355-2

Printed in the United States of America

Scripture quotations, unless otherwise noted, are from The Holy Bible, New International Version. Copyright 1984, International Bible Society. Used by permission of Zondervan Publishers.

Cover design by Rick Gibson
Interior text design by Sandy Armstrong, Strong Design

Abilene Christian University Press
1626 Campus Court
Abilene, Texas 79601
1-877-816-4455 toll free

For current information about all Leafwood titles, visit our Web site:
www.leafwoodpublishers.com

To my parents, D. A. and Gerry Cochran,

whose explicit goals for Becky, Nancy, Libby, and me were

that we become Christians, marry Christians,

and attend a Christian college.

Their unwavering pursuit of this dream

continues to bear fruit into the fourth generation.

Gratitude inexpressible.

TABLE OF CONTENTS

Acknowledgements...9

Preface...11

Introduction: Facing Our Questions.................................. 15

Unity
1   Why Is There So Little Unity among Christians?.............. 21

Diversity
2   How Should We View Christ Followers
    in Other Christian Traditions?.................................... 41

Homosexuality
3   How Should the Church Face
    the Issues Surrounding Homosexuality?.................... 59

Gender
4   Can Women Lead the Christian Assembly? 81

Lost?
5   Will God Forgive Christians Who Fall Away? 101

Saved?
6   What Is the Eternal Destiny of Those
    Who Have Never Heard of Jesus? 123

Communion
7   Is the Lord's Supper a Table or an Altar? 143

Worship
8   Do We Worship on Sunday or Every Day?....................... 163

Conclusion: Towards Peaceful and Productive Dialogue.................. 183

For Further Reading... 191

ACKNOWLEDGEMENTS

I imagine writing a book alone would be like racing the Indianopolis 500 without a pit crew. Bad idea. The pit crew in this project consists of people who are not only extremely talented, they are also the kind of people I'd love to have as neighbors. I feel fortunate that they were willing to help shepherd my first book from a rough idea to the essays you hold in your hands.

First, I want to thank Leonard Allen and the staff of Leafwood Publishers for making this happen. I doubt this book would have been written without the early enthusiasm Leonard expressed for the idea.

I am humbled by and grateful for the support provided by Michael and Jan Seay, John and Anita Henderson, Leon and Margaret Blue, and the elders of the Windsong Church of Christ in Little Rock, Arkansas. I am always amazed and inspired to see people act in ways that well deserve the tag "generous."

I owe immense thanks to Jon Singleton for his editing expertise and his enthusiasm for the book's goals. His observations, ideas, and suggestions made this book much better than if the words had been mine alone. Working with Jon reminded me of the multiple benefits of collaboration, and I deepened a friendship in the process.

Prior to completing the final draft, several persons proofread portions of the manuscript and provided constructive suggestions or caught typographical errors. It's unlikely that readers will be able to detect their specific contributions, but I know. These partners include Alyse Ross, Holly Goslin, Alyssa Abraham, Jim Hoffman, Sara Barton, and my colleagues in the College of Bible and Ministry at Harding University.

I deeply appreciate the following people who generously provided endorsements of the book: Mike Cope, director of the Pepperdine Bible Lectures; Monte Cox, dean of the College of Bible and Ministry, Harding University; Randy Harris, professor, spiritual director, and sponsor of the Monk Warriors; and David Wray, professor emeritus in the College of Biblical Studies, Abilene Christian University.

And finally, I want to thank my wife, Nita, who urged me to do this and who throughout our thirty-three years together has taught me to ask better questions.

PREFACE

Jeff is waiting by my office door as I return from my 11:00 AM class. "Are you ready?" I ask. After I put my books on my desk and grab my coat, we head down the stairs, out of the Bible building, and across the parking lot to my truck. We are off to one of the numerous Mexican restaurants near the campus where I teach. I have found conversations to be more casual at restaurants than in my faculty office, and I welcome that. I desire to foster relationships with students that are less formal than the relationships one might expect to exist between a fifty-five-year-old faculty member and a twenty-year-old student. University students desire mentors, and middle-aged teachers want to make a difference in the lives of younger people. It's a win-win.

Yesterday, Jeff asked a question in class that I sensed went beyond casual interest, and because it was important to him, it became important to me. Through the years I have found that engaging students' questions as if they were my own makes not only for better conversation, but also for better-informed faith. Jeff's question is like so many other questions I hear from college-aged young adults in my context: questions of ultimate meaning and truth, of doctrine and theology, questions that demonstrate a desire to serve and keep faith, questions that demand attentive exploration. I feel privileged to be entrusted with them.

These musings on faith, shared between myself and searching students, almost always inspire and challenge me, because the questions come from that deep place where our souls store our yearnings. We are fellow seekers, chatting over lunch, exploring questions of ultimate importance. For spiritual stimulation it's a combination hard to beat.

This book has grown out of the questions posed by students in my New Testament Church course at Harding University. For many years, I have invited them to submit any questions they would like for us to address during the course. I ask them to do this anonymously, hoping to free them to ask about any topic that interests them. I collect and compile the students' questions into a single document that I entitle "Our Questions." I then photocopy and return the questions to the class members at the next meeting. I do not purge the list in any way, nor do I alter the wording of their questions. Many Fridays I begin class by saying something like, "Get out your copy of 'Our Questions.' Let's look at #16 and #25. These two questions seem to be raising similar concerns. Let's talk about them." Then I begin the dialogue: (1) "What do you think the person asking this question is concerned about?" (2) "Why is this question important?" and (3) "Where in Scripture would we go to begin to address this question?"

I find it a good first move to invite students to turn to their neighbor and peer-dialogue about the question. This gives everyone a chance to voice their view (tentative as it may be) and to hear another's view. Then I open the floor to anyone who wishes to contribute. After everyone has had a chance to be heard and to respond to others' comments, I attempt to offer balanced and biblically faithful answers. In giving these answers, I aim to explore both the obvious and the less-than-obvious biblical texts that could shape our perspectives on the question. Though some of these dialogues take only fifteen minutes, if the question is important enough and the students are highly interested, I sometimes let these discussions consume the entire class period. I believe that students learn more from these open, searching conversations than they could from simply hearing me lecture to them. I get to say everything in these discussions that I would say in a lecture, but they listen more intently because they have first been heard and the questions are theirs.

I intend for my responses to be candid and conciliatory. To qualify as authentic dialogue, transparency and respect for opposing views must be present in generous amounts. Even in a university closely tied to a particular faith tradition (mine is affiliated with the Churches of Christ), the students bring numerous theological orientations into the classroom. In my experience, some students hold fairly "traditional" views, others are working from different traditions entirely, and still others are searching for creative re-readings of Scripture. Once in a while, I encounter students who seek unorthodoxy for its own sake. I have no doubt that there can be genuine good at the root of even this contrarian form of self-expression, as these students try to leave behind the faith of their elders in search of their own faith, or perhaps as they give voice to some unresolved personal issue from the past. It is not uncommon for all of these kinds of students to seek follow-up conversations with me, just like the one I am having over lunch with Jeff.

I invite you to eavesdrop on these theological conversations as you read the chapters of this book, to form your own opinions, and to discuss them with fellow Christians whose minds and hearts you have come to trust.

We Christians are on a journey together. We seek progress in holiness and ministry, living and thinking. But we seek this progress *together*. This makes the journey itself nearly as significant as the destination. May we walk together as friends, not enemies, as partners, not opponents, and may the resulting unity give our God pleasure.

FACING OUR QUESTIONS

Questions stretch us. They prompt us to think. (Just ask Socrates, who believed question posing to be the best way to educate). Given the complexity of the questions now facing us, the church needs to think carefully about them. But not just any kind of thinking will suffice. We need the kind of inquiry that helps us face our problems—*and face them together.* Too much of the thought being done today by Christians is defensive in tone and divisive in result. Its intent is to defend what others before us already concluded. We take sides and fuss, letting the need for treating each other right get replaced by the goal of being proven right. We manufacture more logical weapons, more scriptural arguments, more reasons to support our entrenched positions. Thought that merely defends trenches dug long ago eventually produces battle fatigue in what can feel like endless, fruitless wars.

Too many folks are like the person who says, "My mind is made up; don't confuse me with the facts." Rarely do we consider whether our own conclusions need re-examining—whether we might even call a cease-fire. Even if we arrive at the same place again, the process of asking questions and discussing them with others reaps abundant rewards. Not least among these rewards will be a newfound unity and peace. True dialogue can be uncomfortable, but we cannot use this discomfort as an excuse for surrounding ourselves only with those who think as we do. If we conduct the discussion according to the Golden Rule, open and honest questions can bring us together. Some even go so far as to say that true unity does not exist until it has weathered conflict. The church's witness in the world is damaged when we allow our disagreements to divide us. For this reason, the tone of the conversation as we explore the questions together may be as important as the conclusions we reach.

As Christians, though, we have tended to be better at believing than we have been at careful thinking. We have sometimes opted to settle for glib and easy answers. Questions generate uneasiness. Answers soothe us. Answers close the window to additional perspectives, as if the breeze of inquiry is no longer needed now that a conclusion has been reached. Relying on church leaders to tell us the right answers seemed to work as long as our surrounding culture seemed stable and supportive. But today both our knowledge and our ways of knowing it are being challenged. Our nation's cultural values are increasingly anti-Christian. Today Christianity is limping, having been wounded by a culture that previously felt like an ally. But it has also been wounded, at least some of the time, by our own infighting.

We are not in Kansas anymore, as evidenced by the complexity of the questions the church today needs to consider. But to question our beliefs, to open ourselves up to other possible ways of seeing and being, is to risk having to change. And change is usually painful, including (and maybe especially) changing our religious beliefs. Our fears beg us not to take this risk. And those who listen to their fears will choose to retreat to the comfort of their unchallenged conclusions. It's a meager comfort, though, the comfort of the trenches: cold, lonely, full of mud and old, bad blood.

Questions call us out. Questions push us to consider other options. Questions bring us face-to-face with each other. Of course, it is true that sometimes when we have dared to question, we have ended up more divided than ever. When we ask questions, we risk disagreement. From one point of view, our divisions are understandable. It can be uncomfortable to sit with those with whom we disagree and listen to their perspective. True listening requires discipline and compassion. What's more, some questions have no answers. They cannot be solved and put back on the shelf. They remain with us, pulling on our sleeves, prompting us to engage them again and again.

In that way questions are life-giving. So we need questions of all kinds: questions with answers that lead us to new knowledge; irresolvable questions that remind us that ambiguity and complexity cannot always be removed; interpretive questions that sharpen our perceptions of truth and call us to deeper places of wisdom, dialogue, and fellowship. This book tries to give a fair hearing to all these kinds of questions.

Questions help us clarify our own opinions. But when our opinions differ, when we cannot agree, and no amount of dialogue will move us to the other's side, what then? Must we lose respect for each other? Must we dig in and fight? Does asking the tough questions inevitably lead to distrust or division? There must be a way to discuss our differences while demonstrating the love and preserving the unity to which Jesus calls us—a way to disagree but not divide. *How we treat each other while we differ is as important as resolving our differences.*

My sense is that many of us understand Scripture better than we understand each other. We have so valued orthodoxy that we have given ourselves permission to devalue those we consider unorthodox, people (right or wrong) for whom Christ died. We have not been very good at respecting those with whom we disagree, because we cannot see from their perspective nor accept their sincerity. We have discovered what we believe, so we think we can stop listening. My hope in this book is for the Bible's clear teaching about unity to be as important to us as any other topic. Our Bible study can bring us back together if we search with humility, accepting that other faithful searchers may not reach *our* conclusions.

In the church, too often, questions are discouraged. If we ask questions, we often feel like we are challenging our leaders, or the heroes of faith who have gone before. To question is to challenge what has already been decided or concluded, and to risk discovering that even long-standing conclusions might have less support in Scripture than we assumed. We fear questions, either because we do not know how to respond to them, or because we fear how others will react to them, or because we fear that our present doctrinal conclusions cannot withstand them. Consequently, anyone daring to pose questions might be viewed with suspicion.

The church's life, health, and work depend on its irreducible diversity, as Paul pointed out when he compared the church to a human body with its various parts (1 Cor. 12:12–27). For example, Paul says the ear cannot assume that because it is not an eye it does not belong to the body. The body is diverse, and its diversity is advantageous. Permeating its diversity, however, there is unity. Diversity within unity, and unity in spite of our diversity.

Why would we assume diversity in the body of Christ includes diversity of function, but not also diversity of interpretation? Paul begins the extended treatment of the body metaphor in 1 Corinthians 12:12–27 by noting that this one body consists of Jews and Gentiles, slaves and free. How likely is it that Jews and Gentiles agreed about everything or interpreted the Scriptures in the same way? The body of Christ possesses a range of viewpoints and opinions about dozens of issues regarding what we should believe and practice. That diversity is not going away. Perhaps we should embrace it, welcoming it as part of the cross Jesus calls us to bear. When we submit ourselves to the difficulty of working with fellow Christians whose views irritate us, we demonstrate our commitment to preserve the unity of the Spirit and to build up the body of Christ. Let the diversity of Christ's church be revealed and celebrated as we explore our questions together. When we stop asking questions in church or when we do not allow space for others to ask them, we destroy our diversity. Our unity decays into an uneasy and superficial conformity.

Despite Jesus' passionate prayer for unity in John 17, and despite the frequent emphasis Paul gave to peace and unity in his letters, Christians continue to let their differences divide the body of Christ. A primary claim of this book is that our differences on most issues can co-exist in peace, especially when we bring our honest questions out into the open and search the Scriptures together as a loving family. Even when our differences cannot be resolved, we can preserve our unity by treating each other with respect and grace. If the Golden Rule rules our dialogue, open and honest questions can bring us together.

Intended Readers and Desired Responses

This book is meant for Christians who care about the problems facing the church, who have thoughtfully studied them, and who feel a little frustrated or even confused as to why others haven't embraced similar conclusions. "How can anyone disagree with me about this?" we often think. "The Bible seems clear on this question."

The essays in this book are stand-alone pieces of theological reflection for church members who care about the life of the church, but who may have had limited opportunities to sit and discuss these questions with other believers. Each chapter offers an accessible and understandable explanation of the different positions Christians take on difficult questions, and the scriptures that guide the discussion. My hope is that every chapter will prompt two responses in readers: 1) "This is more complex than I previously thought, and I am going to have to think about this some more." 2) "The people who disagree with me have better reasons for their point of view than I realized, and they base their reasons on the Bible." Each chapter concludes by offering recommendations toward addressing each question while respecting one another and honoring the diversity of Christ's church. Every chapter also includes discussion questions for use in Bible classes and small groups, and a separate section at the end of the book includes suggestions for further reading. Both the questions and the readings will aid readers interested in hearing more of Christians' ongoing discussions about these topics.

The purpose of this book is to foster critical thinking and empathy. It invites us to dialogue patiently and respectfully with each other about theological ideas. I desire readers to gain a deeper appreciation of the complexity of the issues and an increased understanding of the serious and sincere thinking that can lead others to conclusions different from their own. When readers put down this book, I hope they will understand that the people with whom they disagree are sincere in their quest for God's will, and that they too have arrived at their conclusions through spiritual discernment and a careful reading of Scripture.

We need peaceful dialogue to replace the intense (and sometimes unkind) rhetoric of the past. Progress in unity will be directly related to our capacity to see issues from various points of view and to appreciate the hearts and minds of the persons with whom we differ.

WHY IS THERE SO LITTLE UNITY AMONG CHRISTIANS?

Sarah says, "Jesus prayed for unity, and many churches claim they want it. Yet I don't see much unity between churches. Why is unity so hard to achieve? Is unity even possible? Maybe Jesus set the bar impossibly high, just to get us to pursue unity, even though he knew all Christians would never really be united."

Sarah's frustration is understandable. She is saddened that the unity shown by Jesus' followers today falls considerably short of the unity Jesus desires us to display. Witnessing our continual disagreement and division, would anyone inside or outside Christianity give the church high marks in unity? How can something so important to Jesus be so scarce among the people who profess to embrace his values? Is unity a failed experiment? Given the realities of our religious world, should we abandon the pursuit of a unified Church?

My faith heritage is rooted in the Restoration Movement that sprang up on the American frontier during the early 1800s. This movement sought to restore Christian unity by discarding all human traditions and returning to the Bible (and its record of first-century Christianity) as our one and only guide. "In matters of faith, unity," said the early Restorationists, "in matters of opinion, liberty, and in all things, charity." The slogan has been repeated again and again throughout our history. But we live with a conundrum. We value unity, yet our history is also riddled with division.

Jesus wants his followers to be one. This is clear from his prayer in John 17, a prayer that is especially important since, according to John's Gospel, it contains some of Jesus' final words to his followers before his crucifixion. We assign a special prominence to Jesus' final request much like we would honor a dying loved one's last wishes. The night Jesus is arrested, after washing the disciples' feet (John 13) and instructing them how to love each other and to live in the world in his absence (John 14–16), Jesus prays for his disciples and those who will become disciples through them:

> My prayer is not for them [the disciples] alone. I pray also
> for those who will believe in me through their message,
> that all of them may be one, Father, just as you are in me
> and I am in you. May they also be in us so that the world
> may believe that you have sent me. I have given them
> the glory that you gave me, that they may be one as we
> are one—I in them and you in me—so that they may be
> brought to complete unity. Then the world will know that
> you sent me and have loved them even as you have loved
> me. (John 17:20–23)

We Christians living today are "those who will believe in me through their message"; it is for *our* unity that Jesus prayed. Since Jesus prayed for his followers to be unified, then, despite all appearances, we can assume unity *is* achievable. Furthermore, if Jesus wants *all* of his followers to be one, unity should be common and widespread. But it's not. What makes unity so uncommon? Given Jesus' desire for unity, its scarcity ought to signal that something is wrong with our approach to pursuing it. What are we misunderstanding that keeps us Christians from enjoying the unity and fellowship we claim to want to foster and experience?

Christians' present approaches to unity are not working very well. We see churches splitting over opinions, personalities, and struggles for power. We see Christian churches of differing denominations never even acknowledging the others even as estranged members of God's family. Valid doctrinal differences make the matter all the more complicated. Still, one might think that people trying to honor Jesus as their Lord might do everything in their power to honor his prayer that they be one. Elaborating the implications of Jesus' teachings for Christian life, Paul underscores the same point in Romans 12:16–18: "Live in harmony with one another. . . . If it is possible, as far as it depends on you, live at peace with everyone." But have we really done *everything* in our power to attain unity?

Unity is not only scarce between churches but also between individual believers. Failing to see eye-to-eye on matters of doctrine and church practice, Christians are giving themselves permission to forego unity with one another. This chapter's major contention is that all of us have been buying into a flawed assumption: we have thought that Christians must agree with each other on most, if not all, matters of faith and practice before they can enjoy fellowship together in Christ.

Challenging that assumption in no way requires us to abandon the importance of sound doctrine and practice. We can all agree that the pursuit of sound doctrine and practice is an important component of remaining faithful to Christ and effective in the work he wants us to do. Maintaining that Christians can find unity even before their differences are worked out merely acknowledges that we are united, in the first place, by something deeper than mental assent or congregational behaviors. We are united by Christ. But how do we attain unity here on the ground, amid doctrinal debates and contentious practices? Must unity between you and me be based on my getting you to agree with me, or conversely, you persuading me to agree with you? Perhaps this very approach to unity as argument-winning explains its scarcity among Christians today. The ways we have pursued unity have not produced unity. It's time to try a new tactic.

Differences That Divide Us

Christians in my tradition have differed on a number of issues, some of which appear to outsiders to be insignificant. Somehow we still have managed to split over them. In the past these issues include whether or not Christians can eat in their church buildings, use multiple cups or a single one in communion, and believe the Holy Spirit indwells believers personally or guides believers indirectly by means of Scripture only. Today, the issues are equally volatile. Can women take a leading role in the assembly, can churches worship with musical instruments, can we interact in any way with churches of other traditions? The assumption that we must share identical views or practices before we can be united has not served the cause of unity well. Approaching unity through agreement means that I can only have unity with you if we share common conclusions about these and any number of other questions regarding doctrine or church practice. No wonder unity is so rare.

To be sure, many issues that divide Christians do *seem* to require agreement before we could meet together. After all, if one Christian believes firmly that scriptures like Ephesians 5:19 ("Sing and make music from your heart to the Lord") authorize only *a cappela* singing during corporate worship, while another is equally convinced that the same passage does not necessitate *a cappela* praise, can these two really worship God together in one congregational assembly? If your people raise their hands when they praise God and my people are uncomfortable with that practice, is it naïve to think we could co-exist?

Beyond the practical challenge of meeting with other Christians whose assembly practices we cannot accept, there is an additional question: "How much can we disagree with other Christ followers and still consider them fellow Christians?" Those who maintain that unity requires agreement in doctrine and practice may cite 2 Corinthians 6:14–16a to validate their view:

> Do not be yoked together with unbelievers. For what do righteousness and wickedness have in common? Or what fellowship can light have with darkness? What harmony is there between Christ and Belial? Or what does a believer have in common with an unbeliever? What agreement is there between the temple of God and idols?

Some believe that to have fellowship with others who wear the name "Christian" but with whom they disagree is to endorse all of their doctrines and practices. Since they do not agree, they believe they cannot fellowship. To make matters even more complicated, what some view as harmless matters of opinion others see as fundamental differences of doctrine, or even heresy. This latter group points to Paul's statement that we are not to be "yoked together with unbelievers," for "what does light have to do with darkness?"

But Paul's remarks in 2 Corinthians 6 are not intended to guide Christians in their disagreements with each other. Rather, Paul's intention is to instruct Christians to sever their significant ties with worldly values and worldly people. His references to idols, wickedness, darkness, and Belial (a rough equivalent to Satan or one of his allies) make this clear. The discussion is not at all about the church's "in-house" issues. Paul is not saying that we must disassociate from others who profess to be Christ followers but who disagree with us. To use the text above in this way portrays those who disagree with us as the spiritual equivalent of unbelievers.

Re-envisioning Unity

When we acknowledge that the church today is not as unified as God desires, we have only three choices: to give up on pursuing unity altogether; to keep pursuing it in the same unsuccessful ways we have pursued it in the past; or to pursue it with renewed vision and new strategies. Our allegiance to Jesus will not permit us to give up on unity, so the first option is out. The second is hardly any more viable: to keep doing what we've been doing while hoping for different results is, to be blunt, insanity. As someone put it, "The system we have in place is perfectly designed to produce the results we are getting." And the results we have received by trying to argue others into agreeing with our interpretations of every Bible passage are church and individual relationships more fragmented than ever.

But what if our assumptions about how unity is achieved are flawed? What if there was another way to pursue unity that was just as rooted in Scripture *and* capable of producing a greater amount of unity than presently exists? What if the foundation on which we have tried to build unity—mental agreement on most points of interpretation—is not sufficiently strong to support it? What if the *way* we have been pursuing unity has gotten in the way of our reaching it?

A first step toward a more effective approach is identifying what we mean by "unity." How will true unity manifest itself? How will we know that we are experiencing unity and not mere civility? Will we recognize true unity between Christians and between churches when we see it? Paul answers these questions in two of his letters in particular, the letters to the Ephesian and the Philippian churches.

Unity in Ephesians

Paul's letter to the Ephesians reveals insights into the true nature and basis of unity. We can be sure that this church lacked unity because of Paul's repeated exhortations that Christians should experience oneness. Examples of this emphasis include "one new humanity"

(2:15), "fellow citizens" (2:19), "one body" (4:4, 25), and "until we all reach unity" (4:13). Oneness is the bright red thread running through the tapestry of Paul's entire letter.

Sometimes Paul chooses to structure his letters into two distinct halves (as in Romans and Ephesians, for example). Whenever he does this, Paul uses the first half of the letter to describe what God has done for us in Christ. In the second half he prescribes how Christians should live in light of the activity of God described in the first half. When Paul uses this "two halves" approach, he transitions between the two halves by use of a special word—a word that is most often translated "plead" or "urge." In Ephesians that word marks the end of the descriptive section (chapters 1–3) and the beginning of the prescriptive information (chapters 4–6).

> As a prisoner for the Lord, then, I urge you to live a life
> worthy of the calling you have received. Be completely
> humble and gentle; be patient, bearing with one another
> in love. Make every effort to keep the unity of the Spirit
> through the bond of peace. (Eph. 4:1–3)

Note the very first instructions Paul gives to the Ephesian church, a church torn by ethnic division: humility, gentleness, patience, love— these attitudes lay the groundwork for the Ephesian Christians' unity in one body, one Spirit, one hope, one Lord, one faith, one baptism, and one God and Father in the verses that follow (4:4–6). These dispositions are essential to "keep the unity" (4:3) of the church. The solution to the problem of disunity does not lie in our ability to agree in our reasoning, but in our willingness to be humble—to "agree" in our way of being with each other. Progress in unity requires us to be completely humble and gentle towards each other.

All other approaches have failed to deliver the unity for which our Lord prayed. The hope that merely sharing common doctrine will create unity has proven to be an illusion. *Unity requires something beyond common doctrine; it requires uncommon demeanor*—the uncommon demeanor of humility, gentleness, patience, and love.

In our quest to re-envision unity from Ephesians, however, we cannot start with the prescriptive material in chapter 4. We have to begin with the description of God's action in Ephesians 2. And within chapter two, we see two distinct sections. The first section (2:1–10) contains one of the most beautiful descriptions of grace in the New Testament. Paul will advocate unity on the basis of this grace.

> And God raised us up with Christ and seated us with him in the heavenly realms in Christ Jesus, in order that in the coming ages he might show the incomparable riches of his grace, expressed in his kindness to us in Christ Jesus. For it is by grace you have been saved, through faith—and this is not from yourselves, it is the gift of God—not by works, so that no one can boast. (Eph. 2:6–9)

In the second half of the chapter, Paul uses a number of phrases to point to the same truth: by the grace of God, two dissimilar peoples (Gentile Christians and Jewish Christians) have been made into one. Note the numerous ways Paul expresses this reality:

- "You who once were far off have been brought near by the blood of Christ." (2:12)
- "For he himself is our peace, who has made us both one." (2:14)
- ". . . he has broken down in his flesh the dividing wall of hostility." (2:14)
- ". . . that he might create in himself one new man in place of the two." (2:15)
- ". . . and might reconcile us both to God in one body through the cross, thereby killing the hostility." (2:16)

- "For through him we both have access in one Spirit to the Father." (2:18)
- "You are no longer strangers and aliens, but you are fellow citizens." (2:19)
- "In him you also are being built together into a dwelling place for God." (2:22)

The two halves of Ephesians 2 have a cause-effect relationship. The grace of God in 2:1–10 produces the unity in 2:11–22. As an ambassador of God's grace, Christ brought the Jews and Gentiles together by destroying the wall of hostility between them. The unity of the church is not a result of consensus. It is a result of the cross. Our unity is not established through agreement, but through atonement or, as someone has cleverly pointed out, through AT-ONE-MENT.

Our unity problem today is due in part to our having reconstructed the wall of hostility. We have assembled the bricks of the issues important to us into a wall of hostility between us. The many divisions in Christianity in general, combined with the numerous splits within every Christian tribe, testify to our propensity towards wall-building. One could easily conclude that we care more about our issues than we do each other.

The ethnic, dietary, religious, and cultural differences that separated first-century Jews and Gentiles are more extreme than any of the differences separating Christians today. No matter how convinced we are about worship styles or women in leadership positions, we have much, much, *much* more in common with Christ-followers of every stripe than did those earliest Christians: they could not have eaten in the same room with each other without their stomachs clenching and their skin crawling. By contrast, we sometimes bicker about each other's unsound doctrine on Sunday morning, only to elbow past each other into the same restaurants for Sunday lunch.

If you and I are to be unified, we must agree to disagree on some matters and to share fellowship with each other anyway. We do not create unity; God does—through Christ. "He himself is our peace, who has made the two groups one and has destroyed the barrier, the dividing wall of hostility" (Eph. 2:14). Our job is simply to keep the unity from unraveling. We are to "make every effort to keep the unity of the Spirit through the bond of peace" (Eph. 4:3).

In Ephesians 2, we learn that unity has already been created through God's grace to us in Christ. In Ephesians 4, we are told to keep the unity that God created, *and* we are told how. *A unity forged by grace must be preserved by grace*—in our case, by the grace we show to each other, despite our differences of doctrine and interpretation. Grace has united us to God, and grace will unite us to each other. A humble Jesus delivered that grace to us. Humble disciples of Jesus will express that grace to each other. We must let a spirit of grace *towards* each other trump our differences *with* each other. Grace *to* us. Grace *in* us. Grace *through* us. Grace *between* us.

Unity in Philippians

Many readers of Philippians see its frequent repetition of the word "rejoice" and assume that joy is the primary theme of the letter. But a good case can be made that the primary theme of Philippians is actually how Christians should deal with interpersonal conflict. Three primary pieces of evidence support this claim.

The first evidence is supplied by Paul's placement of the word "urge" in 4:2. Some Bible scholars believe this word in ancient correspondence signals the main point of a letter. Paul instructs two women in the Philippian church to reconcile: "I plead with Euodia and I plead with Syntyche to be of the same mind in the Lord" (Phil. 4:2). The English Standard Version says, "to agree in the Lord." As noted above, the word also occurs in Ephesians 4:1. If "urge" marks the primary idea of a letter, the main point of Ephesians would be that Christians are to live up to what God has called them to. Even if the word "urge" does not signal the main point of Philippians, it at least identifies the conflict between these two sisters as a central concern.

A second piece of evidence that Philippians is primarily about resolving conflict is Paul's frequent use of the Greek word *phronēte* (pronounced, "fro-náy-tay"). This is the same word translated "agree" or "have the same mind" in 4:2. Here are some additional examples of its use in this letter:

- "make my joy complete by **being like-minded**. . . ." (Phil. 2:2)
- "having the same love, being one in spirit and of **one mind.**" (Phil. 2:2)
- "have the **same mindset** as Christ Jesus." (Phil. 2:5)
- "All of us, then, who are mature should take such a **view** of things." (Phil. 3:15)
- "And if on some point you **think** differently, that too God will make clear to you." (Phil. 3:15)
- "I rejoiced greatly in the Lord that at last you renewed your **concern** for me. Indeed, you were **concerned**, but you had no opportunity to show it." (Phil. 4:10)

Some observations will help us understand what Paul intends to convey with his use of *phronete* in Philippians. First, the encouragement we derive from being united to Christ (2:1) is to lead us to be of one mind, united to each other (2:2). This links our relationship with Christ to our relationships with each other. Our relationships with each other are to mirror our relationship with Christ.

Second, Paul tells the Philippians to be of "one mind" (2:2) and "to agree" (4:2). At first glance, we might focus on the words "same mind" or "agree" and assume Paul means the same thing we mean when we use those words in our context. As we use the word "agree," it means to see things in the same way, to share a common opinion. If I claim the best NFL quarterback of all time is Peyton Manning and you also believe he is, then we agree. But note Paul's use of *phronete* in 2:5 to refer to the "attitude" of Christ. Here Paul clearly is not referring to an opinion held by Christ. Rather, he is referring to a demeanor *of* Christ, which the following verses will reveal to be humility, a humility leading to self-sacrifice.

A third observation regarding Paul's use of *phronete* is found in Philippians 4:2. Paul is urging these two sisters in Christ to agree. But he is decisively *not* asking them to change their opinions merely because he has told them to. We know he cannot mean this partly because we know this is not how things work in reality. If you disagree with me, my simply telling you, "Agree with me," will not change your opinion. If you disagree that Manning is the best quarterback, you will have your own reasons for your disagreement. I may be able to get you to agree with me, but that would require my building a case in order to convince you to adopt my opinion. We have to persuade people to change their minds. We cannot merely insist they do and expect them to do so. Nor can we change their minds by demanding or by bullying them. That is not how personal views are altered. So, whatever Paul means in Philippians 4:2 for these two Christians sisters to do, we can assume that he is not expecting them merely to alter their opinions in order to arrive at a common view. By asking them to "be of the same mind," he is calling both women out of their opinionated stances and into a deeper unity, a unity rooted in something more vital than mental agreement. This interpretation is supported by Paul's use of the word *phronete* in Romans 12. There the word clearly refers to one's attitude, not one's opinions.

- "For by the grace given me I say to every one of you: Do not **think** of yourself more highly than you ought, but rather

think of yourself with **sober judgment**, in accordance with the faith God has distributed to each of you." (12:3)

- "Live in **harmony** with one another. Do **not** be **proud**, but be willing to associate with people of low position. Do **not** be **conceited**." (12:16)

There is a third piece of evidence to support the view that Paul writes Philippians to resolve interpersonal conflict. Scholars believe that in 2:5–11, Paul is using words that belong to an early Christian hymn. As we attempt to understand Paul's message we have to wonder why he would choose to use the lyrics of this hymn. What do these words convey that Paul believes will help resolve the problems in the Philippian church?

> In your relationships with one another, have the same mindset as Christ Jesus: Who, being in very nature God, did not consider equality with God something to be used to his own advantage; rather, he made himself nothing by taking the very nature of a servant, being made in human likeness. And being found in appearance as a man, he humbled himself by becoming obedient to death— even death on a cross! Therefore God exalted him to the highest place and gave him the name that is above every name, that at the name of Jesus every knee should bow, in heaven and on earth and under the earth, and every tongue acknowledge that Jesus Christ is Lord, to the glory of God the Father. (Phil. 2:5–11)

The central message of the song highlights the humility of Jesus. He had heavenly position, high status indeed, but he chose to relinquish his right to remain with God and chose instead to become a man in order to serve the human race. The Incarnation is not only a means God uses to reveal himself, but it also tells us something about Jesus.

He did not try to exalt himself; he entrusted that task to his father. Instead, "he made himself nothing by taking the very nature of a servant." Jesus fully embraced humility. Whatever problem Paul is attempting to correct in this letter, he is convinced that a humble mindset will be at least part of the solution.

Looking at the literary context of this hymn we see that it immediately follows these instructions: "Do nothing out of selfish ambition or vain conceit. Rather, in humility value others above yourselves, not looking to your own interests but each of you to the interests of the others" (Phil. 2:1-2). Why would Paul instruct the Philippian Christians to abandon ambition and conceit unless they were clinging to it? Why would he prompt them to look to the interests of others unless they were engrossed in their own interests? The most reasonable (and widely embraced) interpretation of this passage is that 2:5-11 offers the solution to the problems described in 2:1-4 and 4:2. The best chance for restoring unity between arrogant and selfish Christians is the self-emptying, self-sacrificing humility of Jesus.

What does humility do to conflict? What happens when two people are at odds with each other and one of them chooses to be humble—to "have the same mindset as Christ Jesus?" Humility dissolves conflict like heat dissolves ice, because humility eliminates our need to be proven right and to conquer the other person. It is reasonable to assume that friends of Euodia and Syntyche joined in their alienation. This likely contributed in the widespread conflict Paul hints at in 2:1-4. Knowing that conflict can escalate quickly into division, hate, and other spiritual maladies, Paul decides to attack it with the most powerful of spiritual weapons: humility. If Euodia adopts the humility of Jesus and Syntyche adopts the humility of Jesus, they will be "one in spirit and of one mind." They will both be of the same mindset—the mindset of Jesus, which is humility.

Certainly, Christians need to agree. But our *first* priority should *not* be coming to agreement on scriptural interpretation—as important as that is—but rather to agree to commit ourselves to imitate the humility of Jesus Christ. We will then be "one in spirit and of one mind," not because either conforms to the other's views, but because both come to share the spirit of Christ and the mind of Christ. *We will be united whether or not our opinions concur.* And that deeper-level unity will help us, as we discuss our interpretive and doctrinal differences, to reach at least a little more agreement on our interpretations and doctrines, as well.

The solution to the problem between Euodia and Syntyche lay not in their changing their opinions, but in their changing their attitudes towards each other. The same holds true for our divisions as well. A primary message of Philippians is that the path to unity proceeds from a spiritual posture of humility.

Growing in Unity

We have seen how Ephesians and Philippians help us re-envision unity. The Bible provides a clear definition of unity—a sharing in the mind and character of Christ, resulting not as much from our own logical reasoning as from God's act of loving reconciliation. The Bible also outlines a process for achieving and preserving unity: we humble ourselves as Christ did and we then treat one another with humility, gentleness, patience, and love—*in spite of our doctrinal differences and before we come to ideological agreement.*

Unity is not a matter of aligning our opinions. *Unity is the nature of relationships that are rooted in grace.* We are grateful recipients of God's grace to us and gracious conduits of his grace to others. Becoming a conduit of grace requires the mature dispositions of humility, gentleness, patience, and love. We preserve the unity formed in grace when we consider others' interests above our own. In short, we live in unity precisely to the extent that we possess the mind of Christ. Growth in unity will require some growth within each of us. Here are some of the ways that growth may be realized.

Recommendations

First, let's assume there is an abundance of unity already, even where we currently cannot see it. Christ created unity through his work on the cross. Unity is already accessible. We do not have to create unity; it is already present. We are asked merely to preserve the unity Jesus created.

A few years ago, I learned a lesson from Mark 6:30-44 that has challenged me to quit assuming scarcity and to start assuming abundance. It is a lesson about perspective and assumptions. Jesus has been teaching the 5,000 and now it is getting late. Realizing the people are getting hungry, the disciples urge Jesus, "Send the people away so that they can buy themselves something to eat." But Jesus counters with a proposal that undoubtedly surprised the disciples: "Why don't you give them something to eat?"

"Good idea, Jesus," says Peter. "Very good idea. We thought of that actually, but when we checked with Judas about how much we have in the group work fund, it was not nearly enough. It seems as if that fund keeps shrinking for some reason. Anyway, we don't have anywhere near the kind of money it would require to feed a crowd this size." Jesus will not relent: "How much food do you have?" "Well, I don't know, let me check," says Peter, a little exasperated that Jesus won't go ahead and send the people to the nearby village. So Peter sends his little brother Andrew on an errand, and shortly Andrew returns with a sack lunch he took off a teenager. Peter says, "See, Jesus, this is all we have. I told you we don't have enough food to feed this crowd." Jesus looks at the lunch and says, "This will be plenty. Have the people sit down." Then, as we know, Jesus blesses the food and instructs the disciples to distribute it. To everyone's surprise, they have plenty of food after all. In fact, twelve baskets of leftovers are collected.

Jesus teaches his disciples to look at their resources and see abundance rather than scarcity. "We don't have enough," they say.

Jesus counters and says, "Actually, you have plenty." Jesus and the Twelve are looking at the same resources. The difference in their perspectives is in their assumptions. The disciples assume scarcity, while Jesus assumes abundance. We all recognize the miracle Jesus performs here by feeding lots of people with very little food. But less obvious is the "near miracle" Jesus performs by leading people in the habit of seeing scarcity to see abundance instead.

Unity tends to work the same way. Rather than assuming we have little unity and that we have a long way to go in achieving it, why not assume that unity between believers is abundant, and then build on the more peaceful, loving relationships that would accompany such an assumption? We can all agree that it is most faithful to God, most faithful to Scripture, and also most pragmatic to assume unity is abundant rather than scarce. Let's be intentional about shifting our thinking and our speech in line with this new assumption. Doing so will affect how we talk to other Christ followers; we will cease viewing them as adversaries, and see them more as fellow students whom we can teach and from whom we can learn.

Second, let's focus on the true goal of our faith: to be found faithful when Jesus comes. When Christ is revealed, we will be like he is; but until then he is in the process of transforming us. Since agreement on every doctrine and practice is not going to happen, and is not even our ultimate goal, let's switch the focus of our unity efforts onto the task that *is* within our reach: pressing on toward maturity. As Paul said elsewhere in Ephesians,

> . . . until we all reach unity in the faith and in the knowledge of the Son of God and become mature, attaining to the whole measure of the fullness of Christ. Then we will no longer be infants, tossed back and forth by the waves, and blown here and there by every wind of teaching and by the cunning and craftiness of people in their deceitful

scheming. Instead, speaking the truth in love, we will grow
to become in every respect the mature body of him who is
the head, that is, Christ. (Eph. 4:13–15)

We will realize some maturity while here on earth, but we know that
we will not arrive at the full maturity of Christ until he returns for us.
Rather than constantly assessing each other's current progress, let's
focus more on our own efforts towards maturity and on our shared
goal of hearing him say to us, "Well done, good and faithful servant"
(Matt. 25:21). Changing our focus to the ultimate goal of our faith
will enable us to avoid getting mired down by our differences and
the conflict that too often results in doing so. Rather than tearing
each other down, we can spur one another on towards the maturity
to which Christ has called us all.

Third, let us face conflict head on in healthy ways, rather than
trying to avoid it. If the church has not weathered conflict, what
we have is not unity but merely an uneasy standoff. The absence of
conflict may not be due to the presence of unity. We may be merely
avoiding each other, pretending we do not have different convictions
about what Scripture says and about how we should practice our
identity as a Christian community. Conflicts experienced *between*
Christians function in a way similar to the trials experienced *by*
Christians: they challenge us to grow. Conflicts *test* our unity, and
working through conflicts *matures* our unity. Embracing conflict
Christianly requires that we speak the truth in love (Eph. 4:15).

In the past, we Christians have too often given ourselves permission to disassociate from other Christians just because we do
not agree on certain doctrines or practices. What if we turned unity
inside out and looked at it another way? What if rather than opting
to disassociate from each other over our differences, we intentionally *pursued* humble, loving relationship with those with whom we
disagree *as a method for creating unity?*

Jesus wants his people to be unified, and this must mean that we *can* be. But experiencing this unity will require our taking a different approach than our hairsplitting insistence on conformity of doctrine and practice that has created the divisive infighting so common among Christians. The unity created by God can be realized in his people only by re-embracing the grace of God and the humility of Christ that created the church's unity in the first place. The church *can* experience true, deep unity, here and now, and we *can* preserve it. We need only to extend to each other the grace God has extended to us, and to display the same humility—even when it is humiliating and painful—that prompted Jesus to leave his father's side and place himself on a cross.

DISCUSSION QUESTIONS

1. Why do you think that something as important to Jesus as unity is so scarce among his followers?

2. What would unity look like for Christians whose incompatible Sunday assembly practices prevent them from meeting together?

3. Think of someone you know who holds a doctrinal position with which you disagree. Do you assume you are in fellowship with that person now, or are you assuming that the two of you must come to an agreement regarding that doctrine before you can fellowship each other?

4. What ideas do you have about achieving and expressing unity with other Christians who may not presently think of themselves as being one with you?

HOW SHOULD WE VIEW CHRIST FOLLOWERS IN OTHER CHRISTIAN TRADITIONS?

Shelby asks, "How should we view people outside our Christian heritage who claim to be Christians? My Aunt Linda is in a different Christian tradition than mine. Even though we disagree about several matters regarding some doctrinal beliefs and church practices, her life is so Christ-like that I cannot say she is not a Christian. Is my aunt also my sister in Christ?"

Most of us know people like Shelby's aunt. We observe and admire their Christian piety and service, yet their theological beliefs and church practices differ from ours. Their radical righteousness makes us want to acknowledge them as Christians, while some of their doctrines concern, even alarm, us. It's important to recognize that it is the Bible itself that leads us to honor others for their love of Christ, but simultaneously to not soften biblical truth. How do we recognize the true members of the body of Christ amid the myriad, and sometimes distorted, expressions of Christianity? On the one hand, we want to affirm and encourage Christ-likeness whenever we can. On the other hand, not everyone who claims affiliation to Christ is actually a Christian. I suggest we use "other Christian tribes" and

"Christ followers" to refer to groups and persons who are devoted to following Christ. This terminology affirms their godly intentions and lifestyles, but stops short of committing us to endorse what, in good conscience, we cannot.

How do we know which Christ followers are our fellow Christians? We want to draw the circle of Christ's church as large as we can, but as small as the Bible does. Christ followers have always wrestled with the tension between faithfulness to God and unity with others. This is the tension Jesus' original disciples experienced when, due to their long-standing conflict with the Jews, the Samaritans resisted Jesus.

> As the time approached for him to be taken up to heaven, Jesus resolutely set out for Jerusalem. And he sent messengers on ahead, who went into a Samaritan village to get things ready for him; but the people there did not welcome him, because he was heading for Jerusalem. When the disciples James and John saw this, they asked, "Lord, do you want us to call fire down from heaven to destroy them?" But Jesus turned and rebuked them, and they went to another village. (Luke 9:51–56)

James and John wanted to discipline those whose perspectives about the Jewish Messiah led them to refuse hospitality to him, but Jesus rebukes them for thinking like that.

The unity of the church is at stake in the question of how to view Christ followers and the tribes to which they belong. The assumption that our doctrines and church practices must closely align before we can consider Christ followers as fellow Christians has produced much of the division within Christianity. Certainly, in principle, there should not be division within the body of Christ. But can unity ever exist on a large scale as long as it depends on our ability to agree?

The pursuit of unity demands that we reclaim as much common ground as possible.

Judging Christians

We will all one day stand before God in judgment (Heb. 9:27), but even now we are to assess the spiritual state of ourselves and of others. The North American cultural values of tolerance and relativism frown on claiming ultimate truth and critiquing others' perspectives, and would have us refrain from all forms of judging. Faithful Christians, however, find this problematic. We can agree with our culture's desire to treat all people well and to show respect for others' points of view—that is, to not be "judgmental." We cannot refrain, however, from making discerning judgments about spiritual status.

In Matthew 7:1–5, Jesus teaches us not to judge others, because the severity we use to judge others will be the standard used to judge us. (On this point, Jesus affirms our culture's value of not being "judgmental.") He says we are to remove the plank from our own eye *first*, and *then* we will be in a position to remove the speck from another's eye. Note that Jesus does not excuse us from speck-removal. He merely cautions us not to attempt it unless we remain humble and acutely aware of our own defects and "planks." And our visual impairments come in multiple forms—moral, theological, intellectual, and relational. We must confess to having these "blind spots" even if we are unaware of what is hiding in them.

Jesus underscores in Matthew 7:15–20 a different type of judging we actually should do:

> Watch out for false prophets. They come to you in sheep's clothing, but inwardly they are ferocious wolves. By their fruit you will recognize them . . . . Every good tree bears good fruit, but a bad tree bears bad fruit. A good tree

cannot bear bad fruit, and a bad tree cannot bear good
fruit. . . . Thus, by their fruit you will recognize them.

We must evaluate the lives and teachings of others, because there
are wolves masquerading as sheep, and there are fruit trees that need
inspecting. Here fruit refers to all the ways persons manifest their
faith, including morally and doctrinally. Ultimately, Jesus demands
that we resist the cultural values of relativism and tolerance and
think critically about what is happening not only in our own lives
(planks) but also in the lives of others (specks and fruit). How else,
for example, could we know to restore the brother caught in sin
(Gal. 6:1)?

The Tribes Camped Nearby

The church in which I grew up was located across the street from a
Baptist church and catty-corner from a Methodist church. I remember well my father attending our Sunday morning church assembly,
then walking across the street to teach a Bible class in the Methodist
church. He did this for many months at the invitation of some of
our Methodist friends. I am proud of him for having the wisdom
to say "yes" to that opportunity. Decades later, these three neighbor churches began an annual tradition of meeting together for a
joint worship service on the eve of Thanksgiving Day. Even with that
cooperative interaction, as far as I know, the question went unasked
as to whether we thought of each other as mutual Christ followers
or as fellow Christians.

Practically speaking, we face many questions as to how to view
and interact with others who profess to be Christians. Questions like:

- Should I make close friendships with members of other
  tribes? Can I date them?
- Should I organize inter-denominational activities with my
  church group?

- Should I stick my neck out and speak up if Christians in my church are saying things that imply members of our church are the only true Christians?
- Paul alerts us to the danger of unsound doctrine. How much doctrinal error can one possess and still be considered a Christian?
- What lifestyle choices disqualify a believer from membership in the larger body of Christ?
- How can our concern for accurate doctrine co-exist with our commitment to unity? How can we acknowledge our differences yet still practice the unity to which the body of Christ is called?
- To whom can we extend the right hand of fellowship? Which doctrinal differences and church practices are worth dividing over?
- Is it safe or is it presumptuous for me to assume that Christ followers who disagree with my interpretations of the Bible are not true Christians?

Lifestyles, Beliefs, and Practices

Determining whether or not to view as genuine Christians those who claim to be Christ followers can be tricky business. What do we examine in order to make such a determination? And how do we weigh the relative importance of the multiple considerations that combine to form "the Christian life?"

To address these questions, we need to distinguish between individual Christ followers and tribes of Christians, and among three criteria for evaluating them. We distinguish between individual Christ followers and Christian tribes primarily because, in practice, we evaluate them by different criteria. The three criteria are lifestyle, beliefs, and church practices.

We witness individual Christ followers provide foster care for children, work in the downtown soup kitchen and medical clinic, tutor at-risk teens, and donate to charities. We experience their genuine kindness to us, we see the respect they display to others, and we hear the passion in their voices as they talk about their volunteer church and community work. In short, we see their faith in action and to a degree that puts to shame many of those in our own tribe. We don't seem to have a problem until we learn that the people living these exemplary lives belong to tribes whose beliefs and practices seem unbiblical to us. We could never imagine belonging to their church, because to do so would mean compromising what we believe the Bible teaches regarding the beliefs and practices of Christ's church.

I remember when I became seriously concerned about Shelby's question of how to think of Christ followers from other Christian tribes and especially how to weigh the criteria of lifestyle, beliefs (doctrine), and church practice. I was listening to someone describe the life and ministry of Teresa of Calcutta, the Catholic nun popularly known as "Mother Teresa." She founded the Missionaries of Charity in 1950 with thirteen members. Their number has since grown to more than 4,500, and they are running orphanages, AIDS hospices, medical clinics, and homes for the dying in 130 countries. Adherents take four vows: poverty, chastity, obedience, and the pledge to give wholehearted and free service to the poorest of the poor. Do you know of anyone who does not admire and commend Mother Teresa and her fellow workers? While listening to the lecturer recount Teresa's life of service, the parable of the sheep and the goats recorded in Matthew 25:31–46 came to mind, and with it a disturbing thought.

The parable is clearly a final judgment scene. The king divides everyone into two groups, then says to the group on his right, "Come, you who are blessed by my Father; take your inheritance, the kingdom prepared for you since the creation of the world" (25:34). He then cites the criteria that qualified them for this inheritance: "I was hungry and you gave me something to eat, I was thirsty and you gave me something to drink, I was a stranger and you invited me in, I needed clothes and you clothed me, I was sick and you looked after me, I was in prison and you came to visit me." The righteous respond in puzzlement not being able to recall when they saw the king in those dire situations. The king responds, "Whatever you did for one of the least of these brothers and sisters of mine, you did for me" (25:40).

The king then turns to the group on his left and announces their destiny, "Depart from me, you who are cursed, into the eternal fire prepared for the devil and his angels." He then reveals the reason they are being punished. They encountered people in the same dismal situations as did the righteous, except they didn't do anything to help them. Jesus ends the parable by announcing, "Then they will go away to eternal punishment, but the righteous to eternal life" (25:46).

According to Jesus, those who do the kinds of service Teresa offered for nearly fifty years will enter heaven, and those who do not, will not. Was Jesus exaggerating? Will the actions he names here really be the criteria by which we will be judged? Must I visit a prisoner in order to be saved? Clearly, not only the accuracy of our believing, but also the quality of our living will be a central part of our final examination before God.

Since what the sheep and the goats believed is not mentioned in these criteria for final judgment, should we conclude that Jesus is teaching us that *orthopraxy* (right living) is so important that it rivals, if not trumps, *orthodoxy* (right believing)? Could it be true that for persons claiming to be Christians, how they live may be as important, or even more important, than what they believe? Or might God forgive some doctrinal error, just like he forgives the moral sins of the orthodox? What would it mean for our view of other Christ followers if we were to give the same relative importance to orthodoxy and orthopraxy as Jesus does?

The case of Teresa well illustrates the bind we find ourselves in regarding the spiritual status of others. Her life of service appears to be exemplary. It's obvious she took seriously truths of Matthew 25. Yet her membership in the Roman Catholic Church poses problems for many other Christ followers, especially Evangelicals. These problems mostly pertain to Catholic doctrines and practices including beliefs about Mary, the papacy, the doctrine of original sin, and the role of priests, to name a few.

When I read texts that have helped define my Christian identity, like Acts 2:38 for example, I am convicted that I should teach Teresa (were she still alive and had I the opportunity) what I believe the New Testament says about original sin and baptism. When I read texts like Matthew 25, however, I am convicted of my need to be taught about ministry by Teresa. On the other hand, excelling in Christian service cannot replace the need to pursue orthodox Christian doctrine.

Who is in the better spiritual position: persons who emphasize correct doctrine but demonstrate little concern for the poor, or persons who live like Jesus but who hold what may be perceived as an insufficient understanding of doctrine? We all agree it would be best to possess high degrees of both orthodoxy and orthopraxy. But Jesus' teaching refuses to give us such an easy out. He forces us to face the more complicated question that arises whenever we compare two individuals. One emphasizes the importance of an accurate understanding of biblical teachings, but does not personally minister to the poor. The second person misunderstands (or is ignorant of) some New Testament teachings but does the things Jesus taught in Matthew 25.

Determining spiritual status becomes even more difficult in that we who are trying to evaluate genuine faithfulness in others must take a close look at ourselves. It would be a mistake for me to elevate the areas in which I have experienced growth above the areas in which you have grown. It would likewise be unfair to highlight the areas in which you have not grown while minimizing those where I am still immature.

Doctrine Matters

Our concern for accurate doctrine is legitimate. The New Testament is clear that there are some fundamental beliefs that are non-negotiable. For example, 1 John teaches that people who deny that Jesus is God-in-the-flesh are not Christians (1 John 2:18–23; 4:1–3). They might make nice neighbors, but they are not Christians. A profession of belief in Christ itself is loaded with doctrinal claims: Jesus is the Son of God; Jesus paid for our sins on the cross, and then he rose from the dead. Of course beliefs matter. According to Jesus, however, we also will be held accountable for our ministry to those in need. This is admittedly a hard truth to accept for members of traditions that have relied on orthodoxy much more than orthopraxy to identify the people of God. It is an equally difficult truth for those tribes who have championed orthopraxy but who may place insufficient emphasis on matters of doctrine.

The book of Jude explores the relative importance of orthodoxy and orthopraxy. Some ungodly people posing as Christians have wormed their way into the church. They are living in ways contrary to the behavior and attitudes that characterize faithful Christians. Jude writes to wake up the congregation to the ungodly leaven of these intruders. Verse four is the condensed version of the whole letter: "For certain individuals whose condemnation was written about long ago have secretly slipped in among you. They are ungodly people, who pervert the grace of our God into a license for immorality and deny Jesus Christ our only Sovereign and Lord."

Jude announces the condemnation of these individuals for perverting the two specific doctrines of grace and of the lordship of Jesus. Their unrighteous lifestyle is connected to their distorted notions of grace. This distortion demonstrates in a negative way that doctrine and living are linked. Jude examines the doctrines others are espousing. Right doctrine and righteous living are linked, and both have a role in identifying the people of God.

The truth is, most Christ followers agree on many important doctrines. We may disagree about how exactly God is three-in-one, but we agree that God *is* three-in-one. We may disagree about when a person begins to benefit from the atoning blood of Christ, but we agree that it *is* Jesus' blood that saves us.

Unlike God, however, we are not omniscient. So we must keep reading the Bible carefully and humbly, sticking to the truth as best we know it, but constantly remembering Jesus' warnings about our tendency to be blind to our own flaws of living and believing even while we condemn others for being blind to theirs.

Several biblical texts touch on the question of how to view others with whom we disagree. Paul insists in Romans 14, for example, that there are numerous issues about which Christians will not agree, but which do not have to be resolved for the church to maintain its doctrinal integrity.

> One man's faith allows him to eat everything, but another man whose faith is weak, eats only vegetables. The man who eats everything must not look down on him who does not, and the man who does not eat everything must not condemn the man who does, for God has accepted him. Who are you to judge someone else's servant? To his own master he stands or falls. . . . You, then, why do you judge your brother? Or why do you look down on your

brother? For we will all stand before God's judgment seat.
(Rom. 14:2–4, 10)

Essentially, Paul says, "Some of our beliefs and practices are prefer-
ences or opinions. You will not agree about all these things. Keep
them to yourself. Jesus is the master of us all. We must each answer
to him." Then Paul issues this warning: "Who are you to judge someone else's servant?" Ultimately Christ (not we) will decide whose
understandings and practices are correct. If he decides someone's
beliefs and practices are sufficiently heinous, he has the power to
reprimand or punish. The point is that the views others possess are
not necessarily reasons for disassociation.

   Paul speaks here about eating and drinking. How far would these
principles apply to the kinds of questions that separate Christians
today? Questions like: What activities are permissible in our Sunday
assemblies? When does a human being acquire sin? (For example,
what is the biblical teaching of the relation of Adam's sin to our own?)
What do people need to do in order to become Christians? How
does the Holy Spirit work in the church today? The task of determining which doctrines and practices are non-negotiable and which
are merely our opinions poses an on-going challenge and is the root
of much unnecessary disunity among Christians, past and present.

Tribal Rivalries

The faith heritage in which we were formed shapes our spiritual
tastes and practices as well as the way we interpret the Bible. All of
us—no matter our tribe—tend to find in Scripture the truths that
affirm us and the truths that challenge those with whom we differ.
It is very easy for us to forget that those who read the Bible differently might be as devoted to biblical truth as we are. For this reason,
conversations between individual Christ followers, and between

Christian traditions, often are sabotaged by defensiveness and antagonism. The resulting warfare helps no one.

With few exceptions, the primary sources of our suspicion of each other are tribal differences regarding issues of doctrine and church practice rather than evidences of individual godly living. The line-drawing we do to discern who is in Christ and who is not tends to focus on these types of issues. If I didn't know what church you belonged to, I might see no difference between your discipleship and my own. It is when we attempt to defend our tribe's doctrines and practices that the line-drawing and tension begin.

It appears our differences will persist. But the resulting tension can be healthy if it forces us to continue wrestling with our interpretations of Scripture, our attitudes toward each other, and our own theological blind spots.

All Christ followers, including those writing and reading these words, are imperfect. Our flaws exist in our individual lives and in the doctrine and practices of our tribe. But how much imperfection can be present in another's life before we draw a line and say, "If you are going to live like that, we can no longer think of you as a member of the body of Christ?"

Determining the degree of imperfection in others is precarious, since we also possess imperfections, even if we are blind to them. Do doctrinal imperfections negate near-perfect living? On the other hand, does a life well-lived in the name of Christ absolve one from sound Christian doctrine? Must Christ followers agree with everything other professing Christians believe, do, or say before they can acknowledge them to be fellow Christians? At what point do our disagreements with others become so significant that they tear apart the body of Christ? These are difficult but unavoidable questions that all of us face. As we do, it is extremely important to recognize that sincere Christ followers, reading the Bible carefully and using their best spiritual discernment, still come to different conclusions on these difficult questions.

This is exactly why some churches have split. Christians on both sides believe they are remaining faithful to Scripture and to Christ. True, both sides have attempted to remain faithful to biblical doctrine. But there is another kind of faithfulness—to each other within the body of Christ—which also must remain in play amid any doctrinal dispute. This kind of faithfulness holds us together in love.

This brings us back to the question of how to view other persons and traditions whose doctrines and practices differ from our own. While we can all agree that the church *does* have meaningful boundaries, we can also agree that those boundaries must allow for *some* degree of difference in understanding and practice. We can agree that unity, love, humility, and faithfulness to the truth are essential to the church. The same principles that require us to work together for Christ within our congregations, despite slight differences of belief, can help us rethink our view of other groups who claim to follow Christ.

Has Anyone Seen Grace?

Matthew 20:1-16 contains the parable Jesus told about a vineyard owner who goes to the marketplace several times during the same day to hire laborers. The first ones hired are promised a denarius for their day's work. Additional workers are hired mid-morning, mid-day, and so on, with some being hired about an hour before quitting time. At the end of the day, the last ones hired are paid a denarius even though they worked only an hour. This leads those who worked all day to expect to be paid more. When they get to the pay table, however, they receive the same wage as everyone else. They protest, pointing out that they worked much longer. The vineyard owner replies, "I paid you what I promised. It's my money, and if I want to be unusually generous and pay the others the same as you, I have that right."

How does this parable apply to our view of devoted Christ followers in different traditions? From one perspective, the parable is a sharp reminder that Christ may place a higher value on the "fruit" of other Christ followers and tribes than our tribe does. What if God is as generous with his grace to some Christ followers as the vineyard owner was to those who worked only an hour? What if God surprises us by forgiving more of others' deficiencies in lifestyle, beliefs, and practices than we think is merited? For example, what if God is as liberal with grace towards those whose orthodoxy is questionable as he is towards those who possess what we take to be more accurate understandings of his will? The grace we receive from God is the same grace we must extend to others.

On the other hand, though God may be surprisingly generous with his grace, this in no way minimizes our responsibility to search the Scriptures for God's expectations of us—doctrinally as well as morally. In no way do we need to dispense with boundaries or discussions about them; yet we can all agree that none of us obeys God perfectly. Any claim of perfection regarding living and believing is arrogant and inaccurate. Ironically, the claim to perfection *is* the imperfection.

The assumption that everyone who is sincere in the search for truth will interpret the Bible alike has proven historically to be naïve and misguided. As a basis for unity, it has failed. Even those who are committed to abandoning human traditions and to following the Bible alone come to sharply different conclusions about what the Bible is calling us to believe and do. The stalemate that currently exists between different tribes of Christians, whether we communicate combatively or stop communicating altogether, is damaging the world's perception of the church and of the gospel. And it's at least possible that God intends our different understandings of the Bible to help us attune our ears to the nuances of what the Bible has really been saying all along, so we can all "have ears to hear."

It is time to try a different approach. We are all attempting to follow Christ. We assist each other as we can, and we humbly receive the help offered by others on the path. What if we spent less time focusing on others' errors and more time encouraging and affirming what is right about their attempts to live the Christian life? Partners help and encourage each other. Those who only highlight the errors of others forfeit the credibility that could otherwise lead others to welcome their insights.

Perhaps the most promising option for viewing Christians outside one's own faith heritage is to say, "They, like us, are 'on the road.' We all have progress yet to make. Let us emphasize what we have in common and walk together, shoulder-to-shoulder, as we talk about our differences." This approach benefits everyone involved. It is also the most promising way to examine our differences peacefully and productively, as well as ensure the best chance for our own views to earn a hearing from those who presently disagree with us.

It will be a tough conversation, but we cannot abandon it. Perhaps the following recommendations will help us converse more productively and Christianly.

Recommendations

First, let's turn to other Christians "on the trail" and initiate dialogue. Our convictions about truth demand that we do so. Why not say, "Why don't we focus first on what we have in common? After we have come to appreciate each other's genuine love for Christ, we will be in a better place to discuss our doctrinal differences." Appreciation rather than suspicion should be our initial attitude towards those with whom we differ. Agreeing to dialogue with others in no way detracts from our obligation to advocate the convictions we have formed from our study of Scripture. Those conversations can lead to teaching and learning opportunities. We must, however, allow our teaching and learning to reflect the humility that we have also learned from the Bible. In other words, the demeanor we manifest *as* we teach, and the content of *what* we teach, are both important—and we must obey the Bible equally on both fronts.

Second, James reminds us, "We all stumble in many ways" (James 3:1). Let's be as gracious to others as we trust God will be to us. Let's also be as gracious to others about what we perceive to be their erroneous beliefs and practices as we are gracious to ourselves about our own sins. We also need to be careful that we are not selective and inconsistent in the biblical texts we use to judge others and the ones we use to judge ourselves. As Shakespeare said, "The eye can see others, but it sees not itself." Why would we think God will forgive us whose error might be materialism, prejudice, arrogance, or selfishness, but not forgive someone else whose error lies in their understanding of Scripture? It is crucial to recognize that those of us who think our fellow Christians need to be a lot more open to other "tribes" need to be careful here. We need to extend as much grace to those inside our tribe who believe the boundaries of the church are clear and narrowly drawn as we extend to those outside our tribe.

Third, let's be humble in assessing our own righteousness and knowledge. Paul affirms that our knowledge, for now, will be only partial. "We know in part," he says (1 Cor. 13:9). This is not to minimize what we know. But as we act on our best current knowledge, we affirm that our knowledge is less than complete or perfect. Humility says, "This is what I think; what do you think? What knowledge do I have that you need to hear? What knowledge do you have that I need to hear?"

Perhaps an image will help us here. Imagine star-gazing while standing in a pasture with a friend on a clear night. A productive conversation could go something like this: "Do you see that constellation there? It's called the Pleiades. It's one of my favorites because it's so small and easy to overlook, but the stars are so bright and blue. If you look closely you can even see a blue glow surrounding them, a nebula or something. It makes me wish I had a telescope so I could look even closer. What do you see? Which constellations do you know about?" There the two of you stand, shoulder-to-shoulder, in a mutually beneficial conversation about something you both value and enjoy.

The side-by-side posture fosters a conciliatory, mutually beneficial dialogue. In addition, this posture is likely to make both of you into better star-gazers, as you help each other pay more careful attention to the glories shining above you, as you sharpen each other's vision to see more clearly. It gives each a deeper love for the thing being studied, a deeper drive to keep watching and searching and learning.

In contrast, think of the posture of fighters in a boxing ring. They stand face-to-face with fists raised, simultaneously playing offense and defense. Quickly and predictably, the combat begins. If we approach those with different doctrinal beliefs from that kind of posture, our encounters will become combative just as quickly. And when the fighting begins, the thinking stops.

Shoulder-to-shoulder is better than fists-to-fists when exploring our differences with other Christ followers. I mean this quite literally, as a practical recommendation for keeping peace during difficult conversations. When we must have a potentially tense conversation about differing beliefs or doctrine, we might do well to take a walk together or go on a drive. When conducted shoulder-to-shoulder or side-by-side, the conversation can be less defensive and more productive. Imagine the benefits to everyone if all of us Christ followers stood together, looking into the night sky of our common faith, pointing out to each other the "constellations" that we know and love, but also listening to what they have learned.

Peter wrote, "Always be prepared to give an answer to everyone who asks you to give the reason for the hope that you have. But do this with gentleness and respect. . . ." (1 Pet. 3:15). The respectful and gentle exchange of perspectives is important, not only because it is right to conduct conversations about faith respectfully and gently, but also because that is the most promising way for our convictions to be heard by others. Even those of us who are most certain that Christ followers outside our tribe should not be counted as genuine "Christians" can agree that we ought to take whatever approach is most likely to encourage people to embrace truth.

DISCUSSION QUESTIONS

1. Can you name an individual or group who expresses their allegiance to Jesus in ways that inspire or convict you?

2. Recall a time when you had a religious discussion with someone in which you disagreed. What was the discussion about? How did it go? Looking back on it now, how would you have conducted the conversation differently?

3. If you knew you were going to have a conversation with someone from a different tribe than your own, how would you prepare for it?

4. Imagine talking with a friend in the break room at work. The conversation turns to your lives of faith. Your friend observes, "Though we both say we are Christians, our churches have quite a few significant differences. You obviously feel strongly about your views. Do you consider me to be your brother in Christ?" How would you reply?

CHAPTER 3

HOW SHOULD THE CHURCH FACE THE ISSUES SURROUNDING HOMOSEXUALITY?

Jennifer asks, "I have a Christian friend back home who is gay. The preacher at his church recently preached a sermon that condemned homosexuality without mentioning the fact that not all people who feel same-sex attraction are practicing homosexuals. How should the church deal with the many issues surrounding homosexuality?"

Homosexuality is one of the most volatile issues in our culture today. Outside the church, the debate centers on the legal rights of homosexual persons and couples. Within the church, many Christians feel caught between their commitment to uphold biblical definitions of sexuality and their compassion towards those brothers and sisters who feel trapped by same-sex attraction. Christians who experience same-sex attraction believe their primary identity is as disciples of Jesus, and their sexuality is only one part of them. Many of these would like to be openly "gay" while remaining sexually celibate. Still other Christians are arguing, *as* Christians and from the Bible, that we should change our views about sexuality. The issues surrounding homosexuality are multiple and complex.

Where do we go in Scripture to learn how the church should approach homosexuality? Actually, the answer depends to some degree on whether we are talking about Christians who are practicing homosexuality, Christians struggling with same-sex attraction, or non-Christian homosexuals. Directly or indirectly, the Bible treats each of these groups differently. As we discern how best to respond to the variety of complex issues raised by homosexuality, we would be wise to distinguish our response to persons and issues within our congregations from our response to those we encounter in society at large.

Four Questions

Amid the multiple challenges posed by homosexuality, the church faces four basic questions:

1. How should the church respond to Christians who practice homosexuality?
2. How should the church respond to Christians who struggle with same-sex attraction?
3. How should the church respond to non-Christian homosexuals?
4. How should the church respond to the cultural trend to legalize homosexual unions and legitimize homosexuality as a lifestyle?

How should the church respond to Christians who practice homosexuality?

Discerning how best to address homosexuality both in our churches and our culture, we find our own situation much like that of the Corinthian Christians. Paul's instructions in 1 Corinthians 5–6 challenge us to respond differently to Christians than to non-Christians. Regarding our response to Christians who practice homosexuality, Paul's instructions are straightforward:

I wrote to you in my letter not to associate with sexually immoral people— not at all meaning the people of this world who are immoral, or the greedy and swindlers, or idolaters. In that case you would have to leave this world. But now I am writing to you that you must not associate with anyone who claims to be a brother or sister but is sexually immoral or greedy, an idolater or slanderer, a drunkard or swindler. Do not even eat with such people. What business is it of mine to judge those outside the church? Are you not to judge those inside? God will judge those outside. "Expel the wicked person from among you." (1 Cor. 5:9–13)

Sexual immorality was so dominant in Corinth that in the ancient world a sexually promiscuous person, regardless of their city of residence, would be described as "behaving like a Corinthian." In an attempt to reclaim and preserve the holiness that should characterize the church, Paul instructs the Corinthian church to discipline Christians who refuse to repent of their sin. Though likely not an exhaustive list, Paul specifically names sexual immorality along with other forms of immorality including slander, greed, and drunkenness. He instructs the Christians to expel such persons. Elsewhere, Paul explains that the goal of this action is redemptive (see 2 Thess. 3:14–15).

Thus, if we believe that homosexual sex is a form of sexual immorality, then Paul is directing the church to withdraw fellowship from Christians who persistently practice it. But we must be careful to be consistent in applying 1 Corinthians 5:11–13 to *all* forms of willful immorality within the church. The church often treats sexual sin more severely than other sin—and homosexual sin as a depravity deeper than any other. We must not make practicing homosexuals any more of a target of our judgment than "slanderers" or any other willfully immoral person. The Bible's teaching on this point makes our response to Christians who practice homosexuality both necessary and very complicated.

For example, it is much more common for a church to discipline someone who has had an extramarital affair than someone who is guilty of greed or slander or who refuses to find work. Perhaps that's because sexual sin can potentially be detected and verified, whereas sins like greed or laziness are less measurable. Paul affirms in 1 Corinthians 6:18–20 that sexual sin is of a different type than any other, since it is a sin against our own bodies. It is less clear if Paul thinks sexual sin is worse than other sin.

Nevertheless, our instructions are clear about what to do with those who claim they are Christians but live as if they are not. Paul calls us to both personal and congregational attempts to restore fellow Christians living in sin. In Galatians 6:1 Paul calls individual Christians to restore gently those caught in sin, while in 1 Corinthians 5:9–13 he instructs us as a body to discipline those who persist in it. Even then there is a process outlined by Jesus as to how to proceed. He says in Matthew 18:15–20 that we are to go to the person ourselves and talk to them one-on-one. If that fails, we are to take a witness, and if that fails, then we are to bring it before the church. We can all agree that it is inappropriate to make anyone practicing homosexuality the focus of congregational attention until this procedure has been followed. This process should be followed in *all* attempts to win back those in sin. If we single out homosexuality making it more abhorrent than other sins, we will not only be inconsistent, but we may also foster a homophobic environment that could lead to a mob mentality in our congregations.

Corporate discipline is difficult to implement effectively. It must be done as a last resort, guided by redemptive motives and purpose, and a process informed by the Golden Rule. The holiness we are called to practice necessitates that we be watchful and pastorally bold when calling each other back to the Christian path.

How should the church respond to Christians struggling with same-sex attraction?

Several of my close Christian friends and numerous other university students have revealed to me that their natural sexual attraction is toward persons of their same gender. The tears that almost invariably accompany their revelations remind me that while homosexual activity is always a choice, homosexual orientation is not.

Ignorance and fear keep some Christians from distinguishing between homosexual activity and homosexual orientation. In the absence of this crucial distinction, Christians who struggle with same-sex attraction may feel condemned by the Bible and the church just as if they were living a flagrant homosexual lifestyle. We can all agree that efforts to minister to brothers and sisters who experience same-gender attraction need to be extensions of genuine relationship, where frustrations with estranged families, the church, and society can be aired safely and confidentially. More and more of us are discovering that we have family members or close friends who acknowledge same-sex attraction. As those we love and know best share their fears, discouragement, and isolation with us, we are learning that there is more to this question than people merely choosing "an alternative lifestyle."

While the Bible condemns homosexual activity, it does not explicitly address homosexual orientation and its causes. Modern research and the wisdom gleaned from experience point to a variety of possible factors that create same-sex attraction. These include childhood sexual experience, relational problems, sexual conditioning, genetics, and family dynamics. Whether a person's sexual orientation can be altered is debated. A growing body of literature can help us better understand these various related issues. The "For Further Reading" section at the end of this book identifies some of these resources.

Whatever our opinions regarding the various issues surrounding homosexuality, we can all agree that in the body of Christ we are to minister to each other with authentic compassion as brothers and sisters, including our spiritual siblings whose experience includes same-gender attraction. Jesus was empathetic towards human struggle in general (Heb. 4:14–16), and he felt compassion when observing that we all need shepherding (Mark 6:34). Similarly, we can affirm the wholeness of persons who, like the apostle Paul, may need for whatever reasons to remain single as they fulfill the covenant of purity before God to which all Christians, single and married, are called.

How should the church respond to non-Christian homosexuals?

Perhaps the greatest ministry challenge we face in our congregations involves the reality that we do not have credibility with homosexual persons, and therefore no voice with them. Christians are viewed by many outside the church as people who condemn both homosexuality and homosexuals. A few hate-filled extremists have created the caricature society now assigns to all Christians. Our stance that homosexual behavior is not a godly use of sexuality is seen as hatred of people who are gay, while our sympathy for their experiences is overlooked or ignored. If we hope to speak good news to persons of same-sex orientation, we must build interpersonal trust through authentic care. Not a condescending, "Let us help you," kind of care, but a genuine relationship of equals. Admittedly, this is difficult as our attempts to distinguish between the sin and the sinner are likely lost on those we are trying to reach.

Two homosexual men began to visit our church a few years ago. We first met them through the Sunday afternoon medical clinic our church initiated and staffed. James and Danny (not their real names) were live-in partners. Older than Danny by ten years, James had a chronic illness that kept him on disability subsidies, and it was financially advantageous for them to live together. They felt welcomed by the church members, and at one point one of them said, "When I am at church, I feel like I'm home." One of our shepherds and his wife led the two through a study of the Gospel of Mark, wanting them to have a good knowledge of Jesus before they were faced with the choice between their lifestyle and following him. After a year of weekly study, James and Danny requested to be told everything the Bible taught regarding homosexuality. After learning that becoming Christians would mean the end of their relationship as partners, the two dropped out of sight. We were saddened at their choice, but we knew they left because they considered the cost of discipleship too high, and not because they were not loved. I was proud of the Christians who were in closest contact with these men. Their gentle manner and authentic care were clear to James and Danny. It seems inappropriate to confront seekers with the cost of following Jesus before knowing the one they would be following. Teaching them about Jesus first allowed the two men to make a real choice between Jesus and their lifestyle, a choice that would have been sabotaged had it come too early in their introduction to Christian discipleship. Their teachers were not being manipulative, but rather were attempting to avoid a scenario where people outside of Christ are asked to make commitments to him before knowing what is involved. That's what Jesus was talking about when he urged people to "count the cost."

Jesus acquired a bad perception among religious persons for befriending folks like James and Danny. But Jesus viewed this development positively. He intentionally earned his reputation as "a friend of sinners" (Matt. 11:19). I wonder how many churches have a similar reputation in their communities. If our congregation aspired to gain such a reputation, how would we go about doing so? Whatever our convictions about the issues associated with homosexuality at the social and public policy level, we need to be careful that we manifest genuine love towards homosexuals and offer to them our authentic friendship whether or not they decide to follow Jesus. We look to Teacher Jesus for wisdom to repair the negative perception of us held by many non-Christian homosexuals, and we find a mother lode in his encounter with the tax collector, Matthew.

> As Jesus went on from there, he saw a man named Matthew sitting at the tax collector's booth. "Follow me," he told him, and Matthew got up and followed him. While Jesus was having dinner at Matthew's house, many tax collectors and sinners came and ate with him and his disciples. When the Pharisees saw this, they asked his disciples, "Why does your teacher eat with tax collectors and sinners?" On hearing this, Jesus said, "It is not the healthy who need a doctor, but the sick. But go and learn what this means: 'I desire mercy, not sacrifice.' For I have not come to call the righteous, but sinners." (Matt. 9:9–12)

With minimal imagination, we can substitute "homosexuals" (or any other description of people who sin like we all do) for "tax collectors" and see what the Teacher wants his followers to do. Too often we insulate ourselves from people like the ones around Matthew's table, forgetting that we ourselves are those people. Certainly we need the fellowship of Christian brothers and sisters, but we equally need association with non-Christians. In contrast to going "outside the camp" where Jesus is (Heb. 13:11–13), too many Christians have become inside-the-camp people. In our efforts to nurture and edify our children and each other, we have neglected to befriend those farthest from the church's doors. We have lost our balance.

Homosexuals today likely perceive themselves to be farther from the church than any other group of people in our culture. Many Christians have let their opposition to laws legitimizing homosexual unions keep them from becoming friends with homosexuals. As a result the church's condemnation of the practice of homosexuality has been mistaken for a disdain of homosexual persons. We have not lost our voice with homosexuals; we never had one.

Paul expressed concern for how Christians' actions affect the world's perception of the church. This is nowhere clearer than in 1 Corinthians 6. Here Paul instructs the Corinthians to use fellow Christians to resolve their interpersonal disputes, rather than bringing public lawsuits against each other.

> If any of you has a dispute with another, do you dare to take it before the ungodly for judgment instead of before the Lord's people? . . . Therefore, if you have disputes about such matters, do you ask for a ruling from those whose way of life is scorned in the church? I say this to shame you. Is it possible that there is nobody among you wise enough to judge a dispute between believers? But instead, one brother takes another to court—and this in front of unbelievers! (1 Cor. 6:1–6)

Christians cannot ignore the fact that the Bible speaks against homosexual practice. However, we can agree that the Bible calls us to think carefully about how we are viewed by the world. Paul was concerned that the church's actions for handling conflict not damage the world's perception of the church. As we have addressed issues of homosexuality, have we allowed our concern for public policy to eclipse our concern for public perception? In this case, the Bible calls us to make certain that our message about sin does not drown out our message of love.

Changing the world's perception will require Christians to build genuine friendships with homosexual persons. Jesus teaches us how to interact with persons whose sexual behavior is condemned in Scripture. One of the most direct examples he provides is through his encounter with the woman caught in adultery in John 8. The story contrasts policy issues with personal ones. The men bringing and accusing the woman seek to resolve the problem at the public level. "The law says," they remind Jesus. They create an impromptu courtroom and insist that Jesus serve as judge. The outcome they desire is to settle the issue in the public square. Particularly, they desire to publicly discredit Jesus. Jesus does not take the bait, however. Stooping down to doodle on the ground, he shifts both the conversational momentum and the agenda. Jesus is more concerned about the woman's future than about her past. He desires for her to submit her life to the rule of God. But Jesus knows that in order for her to hear the truth about herself she must experience grace and the protection of her dignity. Christians today must interact with homosexual nonbelievers with the same kind of grace. Grace is the forerunner of truth.

God uses grace to position people to hear his truth, so we should expect God to use us Christians to extend grace to homosexual persons. Paul revealed one of the functions of grace when he said, "Or do you show contempt for the riches of his kindness, forbearance and patience, not realizing that God's kindness is intended to lead you to repentance?" (Rom. 2:4). For God's gracious kindness to lead people to repentance today, it must be incarnated in God's people and in their friendships with all persons, regardless of the type of sin that has entangled their lives.

Showing grace to homosexual persons and seeking friendships with them does not require Christians to abandon the Bible's teachings about homosexual practice. The men who brought the woman to Jesus were not wrong about her. She *had* committed adultery. Christians are correct in maintaining what the Bible says about homosexuality. But if we want non-Christian homosexuals to hear God's truth, they need first to experience God's grace flowing to them through his people. The men who brought the woman to Jesus appealed to the law. In that way they resemble Christians today as we are perceived by non-Christians who conclude we want legislation to resolve our complaints. Homosexuals justifiably conclude that Christians want the civic powers to condemn homosexuality, and that we are prepared to coerce the government to bend to our will.

Even if many Christians desire these goals, however, we know that God has entrusted us as ambassadors of his grace and love. Whatever the world thinks, we cannot let ourselves play the part of the men in the story. "In the Law Moses commanded us to stone such women," they say. "Now what do you say?" (John 8:5). Jesus, however, redirects the issue from a question of policy to a question of engaging people who are not living in the will of God. He affirms the woman's value as a person. She is not primarily an adulteress. Above all, she is a child of God who has lost her way. As the ultimate incarnation of the Word of God, Jesus blends grace and truth in his personal encounters (John 1:14). Jesus incarnates grace and truth to this woman while the men focus only on the truth of her sin. Jesus first speaks a word of grace: "Neither do I condemn you," he tells her. Then he speaks a word of truth: "Go and leave your life of sin." The church needs to re-calibrate its grace and truth meters. Not grace without truth, nor truth without grace, not even truth before grace, but both in the combination and sequence modeled by Jesus: grace then truth. We are to continue the work of Incarnation initiated by Jesus. Is there an area of the church's ministry where incarnating grace and truth is more needed than in its ministry to homosexuals outside the church?

How should the church respond to the cultural trend to legalize homosexual unions and legitimize homosexuality as a lifestyle?

Homosexuality is quickly becoming widely accepted as a valid lifestyle. Same-sex marriages are now legal in a growing number of states. We are not only disciples of Christ, we are also citizens of a society, and many Christians understandably want to help shape that society and its contexts such as schools and work places in which we and our children must function. How should we respond to this trend in our culture? Should we be trying to influence public policy regarding homosexuality and the legal rights of homosexual couples?

How are we to think of Paul's instructions in 1 Corinthians 5 regarding the sexually immoral who are "of this world" and "outside the church"? He assumes Christians will associate with them, but says, "What business is it of mine to judge those outside the church? Are you not to judge those inside? God will judge those outside" (1 Cor. 5:12–13). In the culture wars raging in America today, some Christians suggest we read this as a prohibition against attempts to reform society. They wonder if we have taken our commission to keep the church pure and extended it too far, to efforts to clean up society?

On the other hand, some Christians believe we should persuade the United States Congress to pass laws that reflect the ethical standards God gave to the church. The roots of this assumption lie in the Old Testament covenant between God and the nation of Israel and God's special instructions for that nation to uphold its end of the covenant. We read numerous texts in the Old Testament where God instructs the nation of Israel to live as the people of God should live, and we conclude that we are to live by these same instructions. For example, in Exodus 21 the Israelites are instructed to punish those who commit pre-meditated murder more harshly than persons who accidentally kill someone. Micah 6:6–8 echoes many of the prophetic writings when it calls the people of God to act justly, love mercy, and to walk humbly with God. Understanding Christians to be the spiritual children of Abraham, some among us think we should be reforming our nation as the Scriptures written to ancient Israel instructed them to do. After all, God is ruler over the entire world, not just over those persons who are eager to obey him.

Other Christians note that Israel was a theocracy, a nation ruled by God. The United States, in contrast, is a democracy, they point out. When it comes to governing our country, even acknowledging that many of the founders of the United States were Christians is different than placing the Bible on a par with the United States Constitution. Proponents of this perspective claim that if the Bible is to function as a constitution, it can do so only for the church. Christians will frustrate ourselves and others if we attempt to impose a morality intended for God's covenant people on those not in the church.

While all of us affirm that God desires that all people repent and come to live under his rule (2 Pet. 3:9), some insist the morality described in Scripture was written to instruct the people who have already chosen to live under God's rule. God desires for all residents of the United States (and all other nations) to enter the covenant he has established with his people through Christ, and then to live according to the moral laws prescribed in that covenant. But, as these Christians point out, God has not made a covenant with the United States like he made with ancient Israel.

While we all decry and mourn the moral deterioration of our society, some among us claim the Golden Rule applies to our behavior towards persons who live outside of God's covenant. When we think of living the Golden Rule towards homosexual persons, we may discover a perspective we do not naturally possess. If we were homosexuals seeking the financial and legal benefits that come from being married, we would want these benefits for ourselves. If we are intent on treating others like we would want to be treated, we are challenged to reconsider our actions in the public arena.

Our concern for public policy regarding homosexual rights is one of the more challenging questions we face. We fear the increasing cultural and political support for homosexuality will contribute to the continued moral decline in this country and to the passing of legislation granting homosexual unions the same rights as

71

traditional marriages. But what if we had to choose between getting our way in the public square and the advancement of kingdom values? To reach the homosexual population with the gospel, we will need to build trusting friendships with them. Is it possible to build genuine friendship with people who know you are adamantly opposed to legislation that benefits their lifestyle? Is it realistic to expect we can maintain a strong stance in the public debate regarding legislation pertaining to the rights of homosexuals while hoping to foster friendships with them? We can agree that God's will for them, as for us, is inner change, a transformation of hearts and minds, not outward conformity imposed by legislation. Some among us are asking whether we would be willing to withdraw from the culture wars if it meant we could more effectively reach homosexual persons with the gospel. These Christians believe our energy should be spent winning more people, including homosexuals, rather than attempting to address the issue of homosexuality at the societal level.

We need to ask a better question than, "How should the church respond to the issue of homosexuality?" Instead we need to ask, "How should the church respond to homosexual persons?" After all, it is for persons Jesus died. The following recommendations may help us to respond more Christianly. No doubt readers of this chapter can identify additional ones.

Recommendations

First, let's learn more about same-sex attraction and its causes. The causes of homosexual attraction are still debated, but there is consensus that most people who feel same-sex attraction do not choose this orientation; they discover it. Home environment, genetic predisposition, and sometimes childhood sexual trauma can all be contributing factors, and they can combine in mysterious ways. Attempts to reverse a person's orientation are highly controversial, and at best report varying levels of success. Even if one day we were to learn more precisely the root causes of homosexual orientation, those who possess it may still not be able to reverse it. Psychosexual orientation is driven by forces other than reason, but learning about the roots of same-sex attraction will help us to minister more compassionately and effectively.

Second, let's distinguish between the world we might wish we lived in and the world we in fact do inhabit. We wish we lived in a world where there were no distortions of what God intends for humans to experience. But that is not the world we live in, and homosexuality is one of the distortions. We can begin by acknowledging that we are living in a world where God's ideals have been twisted. As Christians, we believe that situation will change when we live in the New Jerusalem. There will be no tears or sorrow in that city, because there will be nothing to cause them (Rev. 21:4). But that city has not yet come. Until then, let's contribute whenever we can to the ongoing work of repairing the brokenness wherever we encounter it.

A third and related recommendation is to acknowledge that we are citizens of two kingdoms: the kingdom of God and a political kingdom governed by laws and elected officials. Some Christians want these two kingdoms to merge and for the kingdoms of the earth to be governed by the ethics of the kingdom of heaven. But others claim that the New Testament does not instruct us to change our society's morals. It directs us to work with God to change individual people from within. In other words, the New Testament does not teach us to try to make our society and its laws more Christian; rather, it teaches us to make ourselves and each other more Christian. The New Testament calls us to establish an alternative culture to the dominant, political one. This alternative culture is the church.

Some will object that if we abandon the so-called "culture war," we allow the creation of an environment that will become more and more hostile to our faith. Others counter by saying that a good case can be made that Christianity thrives better when it faces societal opposition. These Christians speculate, "What if living in an unchristian culture serves the interests of the kingdom of God?"

Those Christians who suggest we should withdraw from the culture wars point out that both Jesus and Paul lived in societies where the existing governments were opposed to the ways and purposes of God. They further note that neither Jesus nor Paul directs us to try to reform the political realm. They both assume the antagonism between the kingdom of God and the kingdoms of the earth. In fact the kingdom of God thrives in part *because* it differs from the political realities in which it exists. Jesus and Paul both call us instead to invest our energies in the less visible, less manageable kingdom created whenever God rules the hearts of people. Our task is to lead people to live in God's kingdom so that God's kingdom comes to live in them.

Jesus assumed the world would be opposed to his purposes, and would hate his disciples (John 15:18–19). Elsewhere he cautioned his followers to be "in the world" but "not of the world" (John 17:14–17). Peter assumed Christians would be exiles in their own society, persecuted by the non-Christians in their culture. He further assumed that this antagonism would function to further the purposes of God, as these selections from 1 Peter substantiate:

> Dear friends, I urge you, as foreigners and exiles, to abstain from sinful desires, which wage war against your soul. Live such good lives among the pagans that, though they accuse you of doing wrong, they may see your good deeds and glorify God on the day he visits us. (2:11–12)

> Submit yourselves for the Lord's sake to every human authority: whether to the emperor, as the supreme authority, or to governors, who are sent by him to punish those who do wrong and to commend those who do right. (2:13–14)

Slaves, in reverent fear of God submit yourselves to your
masters, not only to those who are good and considerate,
but also to those who are harsh. For it is commendable
if someone bears up under the pain of unjust suffering
because they are conscious of God. But how is it to your
credit if you receive a beating for doing wrong and endure
it? But if you suffer for doing good and you endure it, this
is commendable before God. To this you were called,
because Christ suffered for you, leaving you an example
that you should follow in his steps. (2:18–21)

When they hurled their insults at him, he did not retaliate;
when he suffered, he made no threats. Instead, he
entrusted himself to him who judges justly. (2:23)

They are surprised that you do not join them in their
reckless, wild living, and they heap abuse on you. But they
will have to give account to him who is ready to judge the
living and the dead. (4:4–5)

Dear friends, do not be surprised at the fiery ordeal
that has come on you to test you, as though something
strange were happening to you. . . . However, if you suffer
as a Christian, do not be ashamed, but praise God that
you bear that name. For it is time for judgment to begin
with God's household; and if it begins with us, what will
the outcome be for those who do not obey the gospel of
God? And, "If it is hard for the righteous to be saved, what
will become of the ungodly and the sinner?" So then,
those who suffer according to God's will should commit
themselves to their faithful Creator and continue to do
good. (4:12–19)

Peter's instructions in these texts remind us of the following principles:

1. It's important to know what world we are living in. We are not home. We are on the enemy's property and the enemy is treating us like unwelcome trespassers. We should anticipate hostile treatment by the world.
2. Wild living will be an inevitable part of the world around us, and we will be mocked for neither participating in it nor approving of it.
3. We are to live in such a way that no one—not even worldly people outside the church—could substantiate any accusations about our behaving badly.
4. We are to follow the example of Christ and passively endure the mistreatment that inevitably comes when we call the world to a different understanding of human nature and behavior.
5. While existing in this hostile environment we are to entrust our futures and the outcomes of the world's actions to God, our Father and Creator.

Some Christians may be disappointed that Peter's instructions do not appear to include attempts to reform the social policy of the enemy's domain. Rather, we are to bear the suffering of living in a hostile culture the same way Jesus accepted the suffering dealt to him— without retaliating. The world actively opposes God's purposes and God's people. We must not respond out of natural instinct, by lashing back at the world. Rather, our response to the world must be counter-intuitive and shaped by Jesus' example and teaching.

Jesus calls us to be salt and light, to meekly give up any desire for advantage over others, to live in ways more noble and gracious than anyone expects, to restrain ourselves from retaliation, to actively love and seek the highest good of all persons, including our enemies, and to treat everyone—including homosexuals, whether Christian or not—as we would want to be treated. We cannot topple the Enemy's kingdom by using the Enemy's tools: coercion, intimidation, domination, or anger. Rather, we seek the kingdom of our heavenly Father and trust that in the end, he will see that his will for this world is accomplished.

A fourth recommendation is to respond to the issues surrounding homosexuality with bold action. When seeking genuine friendship with homosexual persons, we can exercise the same boldness required to walk two miles, instead of the one we were commanded to walk (Matt. 5:39–41). We are second-mile people, especially when the first mile is uncomfortable or unfamiliar. In these friendships, we should speak and act with honesty, openness, sympathy, and a genuine desire to understand others' points of view. All of us Christians can agree that, if we are to be faithful to Christ, such a loving stance is necessary, but that it need not compromise our moral or spiritual judgment. We must recommit to take this bold action on many fronts simultaneously. For example, we can do a much better job of affirming singleness. The single life is as noble as marriage when it comes to loving God with all of one's heart and soul and mind and strength, and it requires just as much discipline and self-sacrifice. We need to do a better job supporting our brothers and sisters who choose sexual abstinence and celibacy, whether they are homosexual or heterosexual. We need to give them public support, as a church, as well as private support through one-on-one friendships. We all need these kinds of support as we meet the challenges we face in our own experience of discipleship. Conversely, we need to march boldly into the lives of Christians who are living in ways that contradict the Spirit's desires and speak truth firmly and lovingly into their lives. We must discipline fellow Christians who refuse to repent from ungodly living, regardless of the forms that ungodliness takes, and commit ourselves never to treat heterosexual immorality more lightly than we do homosexual immorality. Let us befriend non-Christians, including those with homosexual orientation. The friendship we offer will not be a manipulative tactic. Rather, we will connect with them through levels of authenticity, reciprocity, and vulnerability that exceed anything they have ever experienced. To do so, though, we must face our own discomfort and follow Jesus into Matthew's house. We sometimes say, "We need to step out of our comfort zone." Perhaps it is better to think of stepping *into* our discomfort zone. We want to be wherever Jesus is, but the Jesus Zone is seldom comfortable. If we are looking for Jesus we will find him at others' tables involved in their lives.

Only someone like Jesus can win over those for whom the kingdom of God feels as distant as Mars. To do this he chooses to work through us. Jesus is depending on us to loan him our lives. As he lives in us we will show such authentic love to those who always thought the church was against them that they will feel it is Jesus himself who has befriended them. It will take truly Christ-like people to win the respect and trust of non-Christians, especially those with homosexual orientation. We must trust that after we introduce them to Jesus, he can give them, as he has given each of us, abundant life and empower them to walk according to the Spirit (Gal. 5:16–17). In partnership with God's Spirit, God's Word, and God's people, we pursue the new creation God longs to birth in each of our lives (Gal. 6:15).

DISCUSSION QUESTIONS

1. In your experience, how have people outside the church viewed Christians' approach to homosexuality? Do you think their views were based more on first-hand experience or on cultural stereotypes?

2. What practical ideas do you have about how the church can repair its image of being (in the world's eyes) "homophobic"?

3. If a Christian were to bring an openly homosexual friend to visit our congregation, how welcome do you think that friend would be made to feel, and why?

4. How did you learn to distinguish between deliberately chosen homosexual activity and unwanted same-gender attraction?

5. This chapter discussed Jesus' response to the woman caught in adultery in John 8:1–11. If you found yourself in a similar position, standing between a homosexual person and a group of religious people who were showing genuine malice, which part of Jesus' example would be most important to imitate? Which would be most challenging?

CAN WOMEN LEAD THE CHRISTIAN ASSEMBLY?

Marcus asks, "A church I know has adopted the practice of having women fill leading roles in their Sunday worship assembly. Women are leading prayer, reading Scripture, and filling other roles that previously have been filled only by men. The apostle Paul is pretty clear that women are to be silent in the church. How can these churches justify their choice to ignore what he said?"

Christians in a number of traditions are re-thinking the role of women in their churches. Everyone welcomes the many contributions women already make to the ministries of the church. (My mom has taught the five-year-olds on Sunday morning continuously for fifty-three years, and I think I'd be independently wealthy if I had a dollar for every meal that she cooked in our home but that was consumed in someone else's home). The debate regards their roles in the assembly. Some churches have women serving communion, reading Scripture, presiding at the Lord's table, even preaching. Others can't imagine ever wanting to become a church where women would fill these roles. Perhaps a few individuals are pushing feminism for its own sake, and there also may be a few on the other end of the spectrum who even refuse to discuss the issue. But the vast majority knows we need to thoughtfully study this question. It will not go away, and the tension it creates will either remain below the surface, though we all know it's there, or above the surface where we can deal with it. We may not yet understand each other's perspectives, but we can all agree it is a good idea to sit down and respectfully try.

Four Considerations

There is a broad consensus regarding what Paul says about women's roles in the assembly. The debate is about how we should understand Paul's instructions. And though everyone in the discussion believes the Bible to be inspired and authoritative, they are looking at the same texts and arriving at differing conclusions. When we interpret the Bible, we seek answers at two fundamental levels: what the text *meant*, and what the text *means*. The disagreement regarding women is not primarily about what the pertinent texts meant. The fuss is over what these texts mean today.

The core question is this: are the biblical instructions regarding women and assembly leadership culturally bound (and therefore not applicable to the church today), or are they transcultural (to be followed by all churches in all contexts)? Two values drive our biblical interpretation and two factors complicate it.

The first value is our respect for the Bible itself. It is authoritative in all matters of life and faith. The second value is our respect for every member of the body of Christ. Regardless of our perspective on this issue, we all agree every member of the body of Christ, perhaps especially those who have felt mistreated, should be treated equitably and honorably regardless of gender, age, race, giftedness, education, or any other descriptor.

The first of two factors complicating our Bible study is the effect of the historical context on *what was written*. The second is the effect of our historical context on *how we read* the biblical documents.

These two factors complicate the process of discerning which practices are transcultural and which are culturally bound, because we can't know with certainty the degree to which they are shaping it.

Attempts to mix these four considerations have produced numerous perspectives. A fuller treatment of this issue could more thoroughly distinguish the variety of views presently held regarding women filling assembly leadership roles. For our purposes, we will use two general categories to represent the basic differences in the dominant points of view.

Two Perspectives: Restricted and Unrestricted

First, some believe the Bible restricts women's roles to ministries other than assembly leadership. I will refer to this view as *Restricted*. It contends that men and women are equal in Christ, but God has assigned them different but complementary roles in the body of Christ. (Some writers use the term *complementarian* for this view.) While men and women are equal in Christ, God restricts the activity of women to roles outside the Christian assembly. In 1 Corinthians 14:33-35 and 1 Timothy 2:11-12, the apostle Paul teaches that women are not to take assembly leadership roles, and these inspired instructions should determine our practice today.

Even within this general point of view, however, there are varying opinions about how much restriction God intends. Those who are fully restrictive hold that women are not to fill any role of leadership in the assembly. Others believe the restrictions are partial, and that women could participate in a leadership role as long as they are clearly under the authority of men. For example, you might see a husband and wife presiding at the Lord's supper together. In congregations that practice a partially restricted model, everyone understands that women are functioning under male authority, and these congregations would not permit women to fill those same roles alone.

83

The other view I will refer to as *Unrestricted,* though some use the term *egalitarian.* Christians who hold the Unrestricted view advocate that men and women are equal in Christ, and gender should not restrict in any way their function in the body. True, Paul teaches that women are not to take assembly leadership roles, but these instructions are culturally conditioned and do not apply today. The two views agree (for the most part) on what the biblical texts *meant.* Their differences are regarding what the texts *mean.*

Christians who believe the Bible is more restrictive when it comes to women's roles place the instructions limiting them on a par with baptism and the Lord's supper, practices the church should continue in every context. Those who hold to a less restricted view, on the other hand, maintain that Paul's instructions are to be understood like those he gave about exchanging holy kisses or wearing head coverings. Few think these practices must be followed today, and the Unrestricted view understands Paul's instructions regarding women similarly.

Another way to understand the Restricted and Unrestricted views is to examine how they compare women's roles of service to the practice of slavery. Both of these are social issues discussed numerous times in the New Testament. Unrestricteds believe women and slaves in the New Testament era were treated as inferior beings compared to their social counterparts. Paul does not unseat these social arrangements, but regulates them as much as he can given their institutionalized nature. He urges Christians to conduct themselves in all the roles they fill in keeping with godly ethics and character. Restricteds, on the other hand, see the practice of slavery as morally wrong in any era, but conclude that, unlike slavery, the gender specific roles established in the church are ordained in the story of creation, where the male was created before the female.

Why Is This Question Being Asked *Now?*

The debate on this question is being driven to some degree by cultural forces that demand equal treatment for all and that challenge our presumptions about the biblical texts that address this question. Some say that to question the New Testament teachings limiting assembly leadership to men is to acquiesce to a culture that has no respect for biblical truth. Others claim that cultural changes have merely opened our eyes to the need to re-study this question, much like cultural shifts in the 1950s and 60s caused us to re-examine (and eventually to change) our social practice of racial segregation.

Recognizing the effect of culture on our thinking is not the same as succumbing to culture's influence, however. My paternal grandmother, born in 1886, did not have to consider the numerous ethical issues associated with the beginning and ending of human life. The capabilities of modern medical technology have forced us to ask questions regarding treatment options never available before now.

The concern for equitable treatment of women has been brewing in the United States for many years. The historical movements advocating equal rights for women merged with the civil rights movement seeking equal treatment for black Americans and resulted in the passage in 1964 of the Civil Rights Act. Clearly the trajectory of these historical movements has come to the door of the church and is driving us back to our Bibles to re-examine this question. Our task is to discern whether the biblical limitations on women are an expression of unjust treatment or a mandate from God regarding how the body of Christ is to function.

Some would argue that the church is one of the last places where women are treated unequally. They point out that the sisters are welcome to cook for and clean up after the fellowship meals but not to lead the prayer of thanks, to teach the Bible to children but not to their male peers (regardless of education and ability), and to host home Bible studies but not to lead them (if men are present). Others say the New Testament's limitations on women's participation in the assembly to non-leadership roles is not a sign of inequality; God has merely assigned to women and men different roles in the church. Some women recoil from this latter view, saying it sounds similar to the "separate, but equal" language that delayed the passing of legislation to outlaw racial segregation. Clearly, an end to this debate is not yet in sight.

The controversial discussion about women leading in the assembly is sufficiently volatile to split churches and even families. It can easily escalate to heated arguments in our living rooms and church hallways. Even if we can't resolve this issue to everyone's satisfaction, however, we can resolve not to allow its volatility to divide us nor to lead us to despise each other. While there are some issues in Scripture that are not as clear as we would like, none of us would dispute that God wants us to love each other. Mature love will protect our unity, even while differing about this issue.

Exploring the Biblical Texts

The biblical texts that speak most directly to the question of women and the assembly are 1 Timothy 2:11–15 and 1 Corinthians 14:33–35. Galatians 3:28–29 also has a part in this discussion, though it doesn't specifically refer to the Christian assembly. We begin with 1 Corinthians 14.

> For God is not a God of disorder but of peace—as in all the congregations of the Lord's people. Women should remain silent in the churches. They are not allowed to speak, but must be in submission, as the law says. If they want to inquire about something, they should ask their own husbands at home; for it is disgraceful for a woman to speak in the church.

What Restricteds See in 1 Corinthians 14

Christians who believe that men and women are equal before God but have been assigned different (though complementary) roles see in 1 Corinthians 14 a clear and authoritative instruction by the apostle Paul. He says quite emphatically that it is a disgrace for women to speak in church. He adds that what he is writing is the Lord's command and therefore should not be ignored. In addition, Restricteds point out, it is a legitimate interpretive move to place Paul's statement "as in all the churches of the Lord's people" with his instruction for women to keep silent. The New International Version (above) places it with the preceding statement about God being a God of peace. The English Standard Version, however, conveys that the practice of women keeping silent in the churches is a practice for "all the churches of the saints."

> For God is not a God of confusion but of peace. As in all the churches of the saints, the women should keep silent in the churches. For they are not permitted to speak, but should be in submission, as the Law also says. If there is anything they desire to learn, let them ask their husbands at home. For it is shameful for a woman to speak in church. (1 Cor. 14:33–35, ESV)

Paul says that it is shameful for women to speak in church, and he prohibits them from doing so. Given his direct tone, some Restricteds are surprised the question of assembly leadership roles is even being raised. Why anyone would not take these instructions at face value baffles them. Some may even wonder if Unrestricteds are disregarding the authority of the Bible.

What Unrestricteds See in 1 Corinthians 14

Unrestricteds are not surprised to read what Paul says in 1 Corinthians 14. "Of course, Paul would say that," they might reply. "He is

87

writing in a time and place when, given the social climate of the time, it would have been nearly inconceivable for something other than this to get a hearing. The way women were viewed in that context restricted the ways they were permitted to conduct themselves in public." You might hear Unrestricteds claim that had Paul been writing in North America today his remarks regarding women would have been different, especially after having witnessed the struggle for women's rights over the last hundred years.

What Restricteds See in 1 Timothy 2

Turning to 1 Timothy 2:11–15, we read:

> A woman should learn in quietness and full submission.
> I do not permit a woman to teach or to assume authority
> over a man; she must be quiet. For Adam was formed
> first, then Eve. And Adam was not the one deceived; it
> was the woman who was deceived and became a sinner.
> But women will be saved through childbearing—if they
> continue in faith, love and holiness with propriety.

Here Restricteds see, as they do in 1 Corinthians 14, a clear statement by the apostle Paul limiting women's assembly participation. His instructions are anchored to the differing roles God assigned to men and to women. These roles are tied to the creation account in Genesis 1–3. Man was created first, then woman, and it was the woman who sinned first. These instructions are not merely historically conditioned, as the Unrestricteds claim. They are rooted in the paradigmatic stories of creation and the fall. While it may be true that in Paul's day women were not viewed or treated as equals to men, his instructions have little if anything to do with that historical reality. Paul is speaking by the inspiration of God. To dismiss his instruction as being merely a reflection of his culture is to set aside the authority of Scripture. And if we set aside the authority of

Scripture here, where does it stop? Couldn't a large number of Paul's instructions then be interpreted to be so culturally bound as not to apply to us today?

What Unrestricteds See in 1 Timothy 2

Unrestricteds assert that Paul's comment about women being saved through childbearing is chauvinistic. They wonder what such a statement says to women who are unable to conceive. They further point out that earlier in 1 Timothy 2, Paul gives instruction on three other practices, none of which we adhere to now. He urges Christians to pray for those in authority (2:1–7), but no one gets upset when we do not. Paul says that when we pray we should lift holy hands (2:8), but it makes some people in the church nervous, so we don't. In 2:9–10, Paul says that women are to dress modestly. We all concur that modesty is important and expand this instruction to include men also. Unrestricteds are quick to point out that we do not, however, insist that women abstain from wearing pearls or gold jewelry, or from braiding their hair as Paul prohibits them from doing. In each of these three cases, we set aside Paul's instructions. "We do not think we are obligated to pray for leaders every time we gather, to lift our hands, or to insist that women cease to braid their hair. Why then," the Unrestricteds ask, "do some insist that we take Paul's instructions in verses 11–12 regarding women at face value?"

Unrestricteds claim the reason we treat the issue of women's silence differently from the other three practices named in 1 Timothy 2 is due to the historical context in which we are reading these texts. The ancient historical context shaped Paul's instructions, and our contemporary context affects how we read them. They speculate that one reason Restricteds treat the issue of women's silence in 1 Timothy 2 differently than the issues of praying, lifting hands in prayer, and modesty is due to lingering traces of the chauvinism that was prevalent in our society not so long ago.

What Restricteds See in Galatians 3

Though it does not directly mention the Christian assembly, Galatians 3 is another disputed text from Paul. The root of the disagreement between Unrestricteds and Restricteds regarding Galatians 3 is whether Paul has in mind gender roles in general or only the equal status of men and women when it comes to who can be saved.

> So in Christ Jesus you are all children of God through faith, for all of you who were baptized into Christ have clothed yourselves with Christ. There is neither Jew nor Gentile, neither slave nor free, nor is there male and female, for you are all one in Christ Jesus. If you belong to Christ, then you are Abraham's seed, and heirs according to the promise. (Gal. 3:26–29)

Restricteds believe this text only addresses the role of social status when determining who can be a child of God. Paul does not have in mind here our modern question regarding equal treatment of men and women in society nor their roles in the church. What Paul is addressing in Galatians generally, and specifically in Galatians 3, is who can be counted among the saved. His larger point in this letter is that Gentile Christians first do not have to agree to live like Jews in order to be considered full-fledged Christians. In naming that reality, Paul eradicates any distinctions of ethnicity, social standing, and gender when it comes to identifying the children of God: "There is neither Jew nor Gentile, neither slave nor free, nor is there male and female." Paul is explaining who can be saved and on what basis. He is not addressing the question of who can lead prayer Sunday morning. Restricteds understand Galatians 3:29 to be a summary of verses 26–28: "If you belong to Christ, then you are Abraham's seed, and heirs according to the promise." In other words, one's gender, social status, and ethnicity do not determine whether one qualifies as a child of God. What matters is whether or not one belongs to Christ, and it is faith, not social status, that qualifies one for inclusion.

What Unrestricteds See in Galatians 3

When Paul says, "There is no male or female in Christ," Unrestricteds do not believe he is erasing gender differences; women will still bear the children. Rather, Paul is declaring that gender (along with ethnicity and social status) cannot be used to determine who can belong to Christ, nor can it limit a person's value or function in the church, including the assembly.

In his book, *The Blue Parakeet,* Scot McKnight claims that to understand the Bible we must recognize the unfolding story it reveals. McKnight summarizes this larger story as follows: (1) human beings, both male and female, were created in the image of God so that we would be one with him and others; (2) when sin entered the world the union between God, humans, and creation was shattered; (3) God did not want to remain in disunity with humanity, so he formed a community through whom he promised to restore unity (this piece of the story is what Genesis through Malachi is largely about); (4) God through Christ restored unity between humanity and God, and through Christ's body, the church, we continue in unity until the consummation of all things at which time we will experience perfect unity. It is this story that holds the Bible together and provides the framework for sound interpretation. McKnight particularly emphasizes unity between human beings as the goal of the story. Indeed, he says, "The story of the Bible aims at Galatians 3:28."[1] In other words, God's ultimate goal is reconciliation of himself to humankind and reconciliation between individual humans. The ministry of the apostle Paul should be placed on the long trajectory that began when God

---

[1] Scot McKnight, *The Blue Parakeet: Rethinking How You Read the Bible* (Grand Rapids: Zondervan, 2008), 75.

set out to achieve this reconciliation. Through his instructions to regulate the relationships of males and females in the church and the household, Paul helped the Christians of his day take their next steps in the larger process of realizing this reconciliation. In Galatians 3:28 Paul most directly declares the goal of God's reconciliation project. This reconciliation will be fully realized when Christ returns.

Some Unrestricteds, whether or not they have read McKnight's book, believe that Christians are to take what steps we can to restore unity in all our contexts, including our congregations. They advocate that lifting restrictions on the roles women can fill is one important step.

What Unrestricteds Wish Restricteds Would Consider

As is true of both sides in this debate, Unrestricteds acknowledge the ultimate authority of Scripture in the life of the church, but would insist that Scripture is always interpreted. When we read an English translation of the Bible, we acknowledge the presence of interpretation, since the act of translating is an act of interpretation. Even the Greek New Testament is an interpretation, a result of reconstructing the thousands of existing biblical manuscripts. The act of interpreting is woven into the biblical text itself. It is also the act we commit as we try to ascertain the Bible's meaning and claim on our lives. Every text, Unrestricteds assert, is an interpreted text, whether or not we are conscious of our interpretative assumptions.

Unrestricteds also emphasize that a view of women as inferior to men was part of the historical context during every period when the biblical documents were composed, and that this reality profoundly shaped what was written restricting women in both the Old and New Testaments.

Several years ago I learned of a church that practices an egalitarian model of church leadership, including assembly leadership.

I approached one of their leaders and asked him, "What led this church to switch models from a male-led church to one led by men and women?" In response, he told me a story.

The church was having its regular Wednesday night Bible study. The participants were reading through the book of Judges. On this particular night they were in Judges 19 which tells about a traveling Israelite. To fully understand this text one needs to appreciate the Israelite practice of offering hospitality even to strangers, an emphasis manifested centuries later in the Christian practice of hospitality evident in a text like Hebrews 13:2. "Do not forget to show hospitality to strangers, for by so doing some people have shown hospitality to angels without knowing it."

The traveler stops in the center of a community in the late afternoon hoping someone will invite him home for the night. Sure enough, a resident of that town is coming home from the fields and sees the man in the village center. When the resident asked the traveler about his needs, the traveler makes clear that he does not need food for himself, his animals, or his concubine, but only a place to sleep for the night. The resident gladly offers to host him.

Later that same night, some men of the village come to the door demanding that the host send out the traveler so they can have sex with him. The host responds to their request by protecting his male guest and instead offering to them his own daughter and his guest's concubine. He tells the men: "Violate them and do with them what seems good to you, but against this man do not do this outrageous thing." Knowing whoever is sent out of the house to these men will be sexually abused, the host makes the conscious choice to sacrifice the physical and emotional safety of his own daughter while protecting a man he met only a few hours earlier. In response to the men's persistence, the traveler forcibly throws his concubine out of the house knowing she will be raped by the mob waiting on the other side of the door.

The brother relaying this incident to me remembered the men in the group that night being a little oblivious to the gender dynamics of this story. But he recalls the women in the group being incensed about how these two women were treated. The women began to ask, "What inhumane view of women enabled such a decision like this to be made? A man offers to let his own daughter be raped in order to protect a man he just met. It sounds like the man is valued merely because he is a male, and a woman, even his own daughter, has little or no value simply because she is a female."

Their discussion of Judges 19 morphed into further questions. "Where else in the biblical narrative is such a calloused view of women present? Is it possible that a low view and the unjust treatment of women became so institutionalized throughout Israel's history that it affected what was written in the biblical documents about their value and function?" As he finished the story, my brother said their journey to an egalitarian practice began that night.

It would be a mistake, of course, to import Judges 19 directly into our interpretation of 1 Corinthians 14 and 1 Timothy 2. Nevertheless, Unrestricteds claim there is ample evidence that a view of women as inferior was present in Paul's day as well.

Unrestricteds would also point to the biblical texts indicating Christians are to serve the body of Christ according to their giftedness (Rom. 12:3–8; 1 Cor. 12:4–11). They further claim the giftedness texts trump the ones that call for us to serve by gender, due to the influence of the historical context on the gender texts. Unrestricteds are not advocating an "anything goes" approach to biblical interpretation. They merely wish Restricteds would give more credence to the historical context of the texts that limit women's function in the body of Christ, and give more weight to Paul's instructions that all Christians, regardless of gender, use their gifts, whatever they are, to serve the body.

What Restricteds Wish Unrestricteds Would Consider

Restricteds concede that women were viewed in the world of the first century as inferior in secular contexts, but that Paul's instructions are guided by the inspiration of the Holy Spirit more than by historical context. They say, "If you dismiss the instructions of an inspired apostle regarding women in the assembly, where do you stop? Could you also disregard his instructions regarding the Lord's supper, baptism, or any number of other practices or doctrines?" It is a formidable point.

Restricteds also wish Unrestricteds would give more credence to the male-female order that Paul roots in the creation narrative of Genesis 1–3. He appeals to this order in 1 Timothy 2 as support for his prohibition against women teaching men.

> I do not permit a woman to teach or to assume authority
> over a man; she must be quiet. For Adam was formed
> first, then Eve. And Adam was not the one deceived; it
> was the woman who was deceived and became a sinner.
> But women will be saved through childbearing—if
> they continue in faith, love and holiness with propriety.
> (1 Tim. 2:12–15)

The roles in the church are not assigned based on a low view of women, but on the order in which God created the genders. Similar to the way birth order in a family often adds responsibilities to the firstborn, the man was created first and assigned by God the responsibility of leadership in the church.

Paul treats this concept more extensively in 1 Corinthians 11:3–16, where he makes the following points:

- The head of every man is Christ, and the head of the woman is man, and the head of Christ is God.

- A woman should cover her head.
- A man ought not to cover his head, since he is the image and glory of God; but woman is the glory of man.
- Man did not come from woman, but woman from man; neither was man created for woman, but woman for man. It is for this reason that a woman ought to have a symbol of authority over her own head.
- If anyone wants to be contentious about this, we have no other practice—nor do the churches of God.

Restricteds point to Paul's theology in this text as a primary reason for their view. There is an order of authority, not unlike a chain of command, established by God: the head of Christ is God, the head of man is Christ, and the head of woman is man. This is not discrimination, nor a way of denigrating women. It is God's way of providing order in the home and in the church.

They wish Unrestricteds would look at Paul's overall message in 1 Corinthians 11:3–16 and conclude that God has established an arrangement to provide social order. This order governs how Christian homes and churches are to be led.

Much has been written on the issue of women's contributions to and limitations in the church. The purpose of this chapter is to spell out the root distinctions between the two main views. We will continue to think about this question and study the biblical texts that address it. While we might desire for our views to be proven right, let's remember that God desires that we treat each other right. Someone has suggested that we can judge the character of a society by how it treats its weakest members. Perhaps we should invite outsiders to judge us based on how we treat each other when we disagree.

Recommendations

The recommendations offered for this chapter, perhaps more than any other, intend to shape our conversations about highly charged issues. We need to learn not only to think Christianly, but also to converse Christianly.

First, we need to discard the stereotypes that are sabotaging this discussion. Some Unrestricteds view congregations that hold to a male-only model of assembly leadership as being out of touch with contemporary culture and with what Unrestricteds perceive to be more enlightened ways of interpreting Scripture. On the other hand, some Restricteds think Unrestricteds ignore the authority of the Bible in the life of the church. But we can all agree that the church needs to remain faithful to Scripture, as well as to understand culture. The cause of Christ will be damaged if Unrestricteds assume Restricteds are mindless traditionalists, unwilling to consider how their biblical hermeneutics ignore the effect of socio-cultural realities on Paul's instructions. Similar harm will ensue if Restricteds assume Unrestricteds are social liberals who casually and arrogantly dismiss the inspiration and authority of Scripture. Neither of these caricatures is fair nor accurate, and continuing to hold on to them inhibits our progress in unity and mature dialogue.

Second, even those holding the more restrictive view will likely agree we want women to have as much freedom in Christ and active participation in his body as possible. All Christians accept the biblical view of the church as a body and want to make our congregations accurate reflections of that image. Why not appoint women to building committees, staff search committees, leadership roles in the church's ministries, and dozens of other functions that would benefit from women's perspectives and giftedness? In addition, words of appreciation expressed publicly to all persons involved in the church's ministries would affirm women as well as men.

Third, let's keep the conversation going about gender roles in mixed-gender groups. What if we called groups together to discuss women's roles or studied the topic in Bible class? Perhaps the elders could assemble a group to listen to their views. Regardless of what is concluded, the men and women who advocate a less restrictive practice, if taken seriously, likely will appreciate having their concerns heard. Men could become more sensitized to women's experiences of exclusion, and the respect Restricteds and Unrestricteds have for each other could increase.

Fourth, in my heritage we have a wonderful practice we call "congregational autonomy." The word autonomy literally means "self-rule." When applied to this issue, congregational autonomy gives every local congregation the liberty to discern through earnest and careful Bible study what practices God is calling them to follow in their particular context. But autonomy also challenges us to assume that other congregations are also being earnest and careful in their study and discernment. Rather than assuming that those who hold the view we oppose are selling out to culture or are holding blindly to tradition, we give them the benefit of the doubt that they are doing what they believe God wants them to do. When it comes to biblical interpretation, certainly those who disagree with us are capable of self-deception, but we *all* possess that capacity. And when it comes to deceiving ourselves, those of us who are doing so don't know it.

Finally, our willingness to obey God's instruction is manifested by our openness to the possibility that we are not presently obeying him, or that a doctrinal position we hold is wrong. (Yes, we all know that *you* are not wrong, but work with me here). I like to use the "Jesus comes to church" test to evaluate my openness to new ideas and my stubbornness in holding on to what I presently believe.

Imagine what you would do if Jesus came to your church next Sunday and made the following announcement: "It is the will of my Father and me that you change your practice regarding

_____." (Fill in the blank with any practice you feel strongly about). "So, beginning next week, we want you to do that practice opposite from the way you are doing it now. If you have been speaking in tongues we want you to cease doing so, and if you have not been speaking in tongues, we want you to begin. If you eat the Lord's supper while sitting in silent reflection, we want you to start going to tables and eating it together, and if you eat at tables, we want you to reflect silently in solitude. If you presently practice an unrestricted model of assembly leadership, we want you to switch to a restricted one, and if you practice a restricted model, we want you to become unrestricted. If you meet in small groups on Sunday night, we want you to meet all together at the building, and if you meet at the building we want you to begin meeting in small groups. Got it? Okay, thank you. Oh, by the way, Wednesday nights *do* count."

How would you respond to such an announcement? Some of us might be confused, but still obediently attempt to change our practice, trusting we'd eventually learn the new way. Others would have to assume that the person making the announcement was a fraud. "We have Jesus figured out. We know what he would say and what he would not say. This guy is an imposter." But if we could verify that it was Jesus making the announcement, how willing would we be to do what he says, no matter how much it varies from what we prefer to do? The test reveals whether we are more committed to being faithful to God or to doing what we are comfortable doing.

This issue is not going away, and the two views explored in this chapter are pretty far apart when it comes to congregational practice. But let's turn our disagreements on this issue into an opportunity to practice humility and respectful treatment of each other. Let's not burn the bridge that spans the two sides of this issue. If we do, we will be left with only a widening chasm between us.

DISCUSSION QUESTIONS

1. Name a practice of the earliest Christians that we do not practice today. Why do we not practice this now?

2. Name a practice of the earliest Christians that we still practice today. Why do we still practice this?

3. Why do you think the topic of women's roles in the church is so volatile?

4. In what ways do you think the historical movements to grant women the rights to own property and to vote have prompted and shaped the church's discussion of this question?

5. Add some more practices to the "Jesus comes to church" test. What practices would you find most difficult to change or give up?

6. What other Bible passages in addition to the ones discussed in the chapter need to be considered in this discussion?

WILL GOD FORGIVE CHRISTIANS WHO FALL AWAY?

Derek is troubled. His father, Stan, was a Christian until Derek was about nine years old. At that time Derek's father had an affair, and as far as Derek can tell, his dad walked away from God at the same time he walked away from his family. Now ten years later, Stan has separated from the woman for whom he left Derek's mom, and he is beginning to show remorse for his past. Recently he asked Derek, "Will God forgive me for what I've done? Do you think the church would ever have me back?" Hebrews 6:4–6 is the text that most troubles Derek, because it seems to teach that if Christians knowingly depart from a life of faithfulness they can never return to a saved condition. Derek wonders if his father can ever be forgiven by God, his mother, and by the church.

Do you know anyone like Stan? Though we are called to a holy life, and on our best days deeply desire to live a sinless life, Christians are still capable of disgusting and deeply damaging sin. But what happens when Christians abandon their faith, live in sin for a time, then decide they want to return home? Can they be forgiven again? Some might say, "Let the past stay in the past," and welcome Stan back into the church without hesitation. Others may wish they could welcome Stan back, but are concerned that they not cheapen God's grace by taking sin lightly.

Forgiveness is a challenging issue for Christians at several levels. We struggle to forgive ourselves for our past foolish sins, to forgive those who have wounded us, and even to accept God's forgiveness. Sometimes the numerous situations in need of forgiveness collide with one another, and when this happens, Christians' loyalties become divided. For example, we witness loved ones crash and burn, morally speaking. We want them to return to the Lord and receive forgiveness. Even before they return, however, we feel compassion for them, having become victims of their own blinding selfishness. We may want to forgive some even before they have repented. Conversely, God may forgive someone we have not yet been able to forgive.

This chapter examines the question as to whether Christians who fall away from God can be forgiven and received back into the church. The question is created primarily from the contents of Hebrews 6:4-6.

> It is impossible for those who have once been enlightened,
> who have tasted the heavenly gift, who have shared in the
> Holy Spirit, who have tasted the goodness of the word
> of God and the powers of the coming age and who have
> fallen away, to be brought back to repentance. To their
> loss they are crucifying the Son of God all over again and
> subjecting him to public disgrace.

Before scrutinizing this text, let's explore a true story that illustrates the bind created when our biblical interpretations clash with our desire to forgive someone we love who has fallen away.

Benny grew up going to church, and throughout his childhood and adolescence he would have thought himself a Christian. Benny attended a Christian college but was dismissed in his first year for a moral misstep. Somewhere along the way, he quit attending church and started to drift further away from his Christian roots. As an adult, Benny lived much of his life off the Christian path. His work took him to other countries for extended stays, and often there were no churches nearby. The influence of non-Christian friends during this time contributed to his detachment from his faith. Eventually, Benny ceased thinking of himself as a Christian.

Decades later, in his sixties, Benny experienced a life-threatening disease that led him to start thinking more about his eternal destiny. Facing the end of his life, he wanted to return to the Lord, but he believed he could not be forgiven for living "outside the Lord." He believed that he would be lost and that there was nothing he could do about it. Whenever Benny read Hebrews 6:4–6 his fears were confirmed, because he understood this text to say that God only gives you one chance. If you learn the truth about Christ and then live in ways that betray that knowledge, you forfeit your opportunity to be saved. "Having been reared in a Christian home," Benny said to himself, "I should have known better than to allow myself to fall away from Christ." He understood the phrase "it is impossible" to mean that God would not permit him to repent, since attempting to repent would be paramount to committing the outrageous deed of re-crucifying Jesus. After all, the language of "crucifying the Son of God all over again and subjecting him to public disgrace" sounds very serious.

The question is whether Benny is right in his understanding of Hebrews 6:4–6. Multiple interpretations of this text have been put forward. Is repentance impossible because God won't permit it to occur? Does the text mean that even if an apostate (literally, one who falls away) repents that God will not grant forgiveness? Or is the text saying that the same hard-heartedness that would lead someone to turn their back on their faith would also prevent them from repenting? Or perhaps there is a way to understand Hebrews 6:4–6 beyond these possibilities.

Some see in Hebrews 10:26–31 a remarkably close parallel to 6:4–6.

> If we deliberately keep on sinning after we have received the knowledge of the truth, no sacrifice for sins is left, but only a fearful expectation of judgment and of raging fire that will consume the enemies of God. Anyone who rejected the law of Moses died without mercy on the testimony of two or three witnesses. How much more severely do you think someone deserves to be punished who has trampled the Son of God underfoot, who has treated as an unholy thing the blood of the covenant that sanctified them, and who has insulted the Spirit of grace? For we know him who said, "It is mine to avenge; I will repay," and again, "The Lord will judge his people." It is a dreadful thing to fall into the hands of the living God.

The passages both issue stern warnings regarding the consequences of sin, especially the sin of apostasy. Both passages explore issues that determine eternal destinies. Like hearing a gunshot, these texts alert us to urgent matters of life and death.

Because our values must reflect God's, the church treats seriously both sin and forgiveness. We must forgive, and treat as forgiven, whomever God forgives. On the other hand, we cannot tolerate choices or behaviors God does not tolerate. His intolerance of sin is evident in the warning, "It is a dreadful thing to fall in to the hands of the living God." Many a time preachers have used this text to invoke fear in their hearers about the dangers of sin, and for good reason.

Was Benny correct to conclude that God's patience is irreversibly exhausted for Christians who abandon their faith? Access to the gospel is indeed a precious gift, and it would be arrogant and hard-hearted for anyone to treat that gift contemptuously. We know from the teachings of Jesus and the apostle Paul that there is a hell, and some will experience it. Does Hebrews 6 teach that Christians who abandon their Christian faith, regardless of the cause, will be among them? Benny's interpretation of Hebrews 6:4–6 said, "Yes."

But what if Benny was wrong about the meaning of this text and about God's response to his choice to abandon his faith for a season? What if his lack of hope was based on an unwarranted interpretation of this text? Are there any good reasons for understanding Hebrews 6 in a way that would enable Benny to repent and meet his death assured that God had forgiven him?

Three Types of Sin

The Bible distinguishes types of sin. For example, John uses the language of "sin that leads to death" and "sin that does not lead to death" (1 John 5:16–18). Scripture also distinguishes sin that God will forgive and sin that he will not. Perhaps over-simplified, Scripture speaks of sin as coming in two broad categories (forgiveable and unforgiveable) and in three specific types: sins of *defiance*, sins of *drift*, and sins of *defeat*. By sins of defiance we mean the choices and lifestyles that result from our deliberately refusing to obey God. Sins of defiance are a result of our pride. Sins of drift occur when we inadvertently allow ourselves to move further and further away from the Lord through foolish, incremental decisions. Eventually we wind up far from the shores of our faith, away from home and lost. By sins of defeat we mean those sins we commit as a result of having lost, due to our weakness, a spiritual battle between flesh and spirit. The war between flesh and spirit rages within our souls, and we experience defeat when we sin by succumbing to the desires of the flesh. We have not lost the spiritual war, however, only a battle. And we will arise tomorrow to fight again. We attribute sins of defeat, like sins of drift, to combinations of our frailty, inconsistency, vulnerability, and stupidity.

Defiance. Drift. Defeat. Wisdom and humility would remind us that we are all capable of any of these forms of disobedience. "If you think you are standing firm, be careful that you don't fall" (1 Cor. 10:12). These distinctions can help the church know how to respond to those who wander away and, just as importantly, help apostates who desire to repent to know more clearly where they stand before God.

Sins of Defiance

Our quest here is to discern whether or not once-faithful Christians who abandon their Christian identity and life have the option to repent and be forgiven by God. We are mining the Bible for texts that address each of these three types of sin with the hope of better understanding Hebrews 6:4–6 and 10:26–31. The Bible exposes promising lodes for each type. Mark 3 and Numbers 15 speak to sins of defiance.

Mark 3:28–30 contains Jesus' cryptic comment about an unforgivable sin:

> Truly, I say to you, all sins will be forgiven the children of man, and whatever blasphemies they utter, but whoever blasphemes against the Holy Spirit never has forgiveness, but is guilty of an eternal sin— for they were saying, "He has an unclean spirit."

Jesus says whoever blasphemes against the Holy Spirit will never be forgiven. But what does it mean to "blaspheme the Holy Spirit?" If I were to do that, how would I know it? Though we might assume that the meaning of blasphemy was clear to the people to whom Jesus is speaking, it is less clear to us. How can we avoid the unforgiveable sin unless we know what it is?

The nature of the blasphemy Jesus mentions in Mark 3 is clarified by a second text. What follows is a lengthy exploration of an event recorded in Numbers 15 that occurred while the Israelites were in the wilderness between their experience in Egypt and their new home in Canaan. The story is crucial to our discussion because it, like Mark 3, identifies a sin that God refuses to forgive. Consequently, it may help us better understand passages where the conditions of God's forgiveness are less clear. This story contains four pieces. The first is found in verses 32–36.

> While the Israelites were in the wilderness, a man was found gathering wood on the Sabbath day. Those who found him gathering wood brought him to Moses and Aaron and the whole assembly, and they kept him in custody, because it was not clear what should be done to him. Then the Lord said to Moses, "The man must die. The whole assembly must stone him outside the camp." So the assembly took him outside the camp and stoned him to death, as the Lord commanded Moses.

At first reading, it appears God is being unreasonably nit-picky when he commands the people of Israel to stone to death a man who broke the Sabbath. The man is out gathering firewood that most certainly would have been used for cooking or for warmth, both of which would have benefitted his family as they tried to survive in the desert, where God had led them. Yet, God insists he must be executed. It appears the man has committed an unforgiveable sin. It is a troubling story.

However, this story's context reveals important evidence for understanding why the man's punishment is so severe. Immediately preceding the introduction of this Sabbath-breaker, God gives three sets of instructions to the people for dealing with their sins (Num. 15:22–31). The first set is for the community that has sinned

unintentionally, the second for the individual who has sinned unintentionally, and the third set for the individual who sins defiantly.

In the first set (verses 22–26), the instructions are addressed to
the community that has unintentionally failed to keep God's commandments. They are told that if they offer a particular sacrifice,
the priest will help them, and they will be forgiven. Next, God gives
instructions for the individual who sins unintentionally (verses
27–29). Again, if the repentant person makes a sacrifice, the priest
will make atonement for him and he will be forgiven. The specific
sacrifice prescribed for the individual differs from the one required
of the community, but otherwise this second set of instructions par-
allels the first.

When we come to the third set of instructions in Numbers
15:30–31, however, we see a 180-degree shift in tone and in outcome. Here someone has sinned defiantly, and that person will not
be forgiven.

> But anyone who sins defiantly, whether native-born or
> foreigner, blasphemes the Lord and must be cut off from
> the people of Israel. Because they have despised the Lord's
> word and broken his commands, they must surely be cut
> off; their guilt remains on them.

Here defiant sin is contrasted with the unintentional sin addressed
in the first two instances. In the case of defiance, there is no sacrificial prescription provided because none is needed. The one sinning
defiantly will not be forgiven. Numbers 15 describes defiant persons
in the following ways:

- they "blaspheme the Lord"
- they "must be cut off from the people of Israel"
- "they have despised the Lord's word"
- they have "broken his [the Lord's] commands"

- "they must surely be cut off"
- "their guilt remains on them"

Immediately following this description of defiant persons comes the story of the man stoned for gathering wood on the Sabbath. We have two interpretive options here. Interpreting the text one way, the man has legitimately forgotten what day it was, but God is so strict and inflexible about keeping the fifth of the Ten Commandments that he condemns the man to death. The second option for understanding this story is that the man knew perfectly well he was breaking the Sabbath but flagrantly disregarded God's instructions. When the man must choose between doing what God commands and doing what he wants, he opts for the latter. He is defiantly refusing to let Jehovah rule his life, and that defiance is described as blasphemy.

Without the previous context of verses 22–31, God's command to stone the Sabbath-breaker reads like an over-the-top reaction by a divine being with a short temper obsessed with compliance. But since the story of the Sabbath-breaker immediately follows the instructions regarding defiant sinners (in verses 30–31), the context makes clear that the condemned person is an example of a defiant sinner.

The root issue is not that the man is holding firewood on Saturday. The root issue is that he thinks he does not have to submit his will to God's. He is not stoned to death because he forgot what day it was. The man is executed because he despised God. This is key: there is no forgiveness for his defiance (the obstinate refusal to submit to God), not because of one specific sin, but because his defiant attitude "blasphemes the Lord."

It is a reasonable, even persuasive, interpretation to assume the blasphemy in Numbers 15 is at least similar, if not identical, to the blasphemy in Mark 3. Both texts reveal that the blasphemy will not be forgiven. God feels strongly about his people submitting to his reign in their lives. The texts also reveal a God who is serious about faithfulness, but who does not create terrifyingly obscure expectations of his people. Scripture is clear that defying God may have permanent and irrevocable consequences.

Our question is whether or not Hebrews 6 and 10 seal the fate of the apostate much like the Sabbath-breaker's fate in Numbers 15. All of these texts identify a type of sin that merits the most severe of consequences.

A story is told of a father's last wishes for his son to develop the property he had recently purchased. Nearing death and unable to carry out his plans himself, the father instructed that the son build a house on the top of a hill on the property, dig the water well at the bottom of that same hill, and then build a barn on the eastern slope of the hill. Upon the father's death, the son built the house at the spot on the hill designated by the father. He then dug the water well at the location specified by his father. But the son decided the barn would be better located on the western slope rather than the eastern one as his father instructed.

To what extent did the son do his father's will? Some might say, "The son was two-thirds obedient to his father, since he placed the house and water well as the father wanted but went his own way when it came to the placement of the barn." Actually, the more accurate answer is, "The son was not obedient at all." It just so happened that his father's desires aligned with his regarding the placement of the house and well, but the fact that the son placed the barn in a different location is evidence that he was doing his own will in *each* instance.

This story is not about the reasonability of the father's wishes for his property, nor is it about the father being a persnickety micro-manager. The story's meaning would be substantially different had the father instructed the son to discern for himself the best locations for the three structures. But the story as told above illustrates the son's defiant heart and the self-serving, autonomous behavior it prompts.

The son in this story is like the man gathering wood on the Sabbath in Numbers 15. Each possesses a defiant heart.

What light do Numbers 15 and Mark 3 shed on our understanding of Hebrews 6 and 10? That depends on how strong a connection we see between the apostasy in Hebrews 6, the deliberate sin in Hebrews 10, and the defiant sin in Numbers 15. The writer of Hebrews declares that anyone who has "tasted the goodness of the word of God," then falls away faces the impossibility of being brought back to repentance. Has the apostate fallen away due to defiant sin or another type? If he has sinned defiantly, wouldn't that explain the language of "impossibility"?

In addition to the Sabbath-breaker in Numbers 15, there are several other biblical examples of people being struck dead as a consequence of their disobedience: Uzzah touched the ark (2 Sam. 6:1–7); Aaron's sons offered "strange fire" (Lev. 10:1–3); and Ananias and Sapphira were deceptive about the amount of money they received for the sale of their land (Acts 5:1–11). Apparently they wanted credit in the form of praise for giving the full amount of the sale price while actually keeping back some of it for themselves. Some have read these stories of disobedience as reflecting God's whimsical wrath that may be visited on us if we make a mistake. These texts have certainly influenced how the church has read the two Hebrews texts. While in life it may be "three strikes and you're out," apparently with God it's "one sin and you're out." God the umpire; God the sinner-slayer.

But have we stopped to wonder whether Uzzah, Ananias, and the others are being struck dead for their hearts' disposition rather than for a single, isolated, even uncharacteristic sin? What if we read each of the above stories as case studies in defiance? What if they are not intended as lessons about God as a trigger-happy sinner-slayer, but as parables about the human tendency towards autonomy and the defiance autonomy produces? God is certainly serious about our obeying him, but surely God knows in our weakness we will periodically disobey his commands. Does God's response to our sin depend on the type of sin we have committed? Clearly, as we have seen in Numbers 15 and Mark 3, defiant sin summons the sternness of God's wrath. But what if our sin is of a different nature?

Sins of Drift

Sins of drift may be more common than sins of defiance. Drift sins are small, nearly undetectable steps away from the life to which God has called us. But potentially, these tiny steps over a long period of time can accumulate to the point that apostasy occurs. We are all subject to this subtle entanglement of sin, like the proverbial frog who would jump straight out of a kettle of already-boiling water, but who lets itself be boiled alive when the heat is turned up slowly. Like the frog, we often fail to notice sin creeping into our lives a little at a time, putting down roots in our character, twining itself around our thoughts and feelings, blinding us to the dangers ahead, then gradually dragging us off the path. That's drift. Christians who were faithful to God at one stage in their lives but years later are no longer, frequently became unfaithful bit by bit. Seldom, if ever, do Christians wake up and say, "Today I am going to begin my journey to unfaithfulness." Instead, they become unfaithful incrementally, one degree at a time. The drift is so slow it goes undetected by the drifter and by the drifter's spiritual family. Then after a long period of time elapses, once-faithful Christians now find themselves in a state of apostasy.

In the parable of the man with two sons in Luke 15, the younger son asks for his share of the inheritance and leaves home. While away, he wastes the money living wickedly. With the help of some pigs, the young man comes to his senses and decides to return home. What type of sin did the younger son commit? Was he defiant, did he drift, or was his sin some combination of the two?

A good friend recently divulged to me that he had been involved in an extra-marital affair for the past several years. If you would have told him ten years ago that he would one day be involved in an affair, I am confident he would have scoffed at you. Drift does not occur by means of an abrupt single decision, but rather through a long series of small decisions. This is no doubt the way my friend's affair began, and many affairs follow this pattern. A husband and wife become emotionally distant from one another. One or the other begins to have conversations with a neighbor, or a co-worker—conversations that start out innocently enough. Over time, however, these chats become inappropriately intimate, betraying a feeling of closeness they have not felt with their spouses in some time. Next comes flirting, then seeking to be with each other more frequently, then gift-giving, exchanges of affection, secretive and dangerous liaisons, and so on, until sexual unfaithfulness occurs. Adultery in its spiritual form begins much earlier than the sexual infidelity that usually follows. Adultery is often the result of a gradual drifting away from faithfulness to one's spouse to a state of unfaithfulness that the adulterers once believed they would never entertain.

Sins of drift occur when we ignore our inner voice that reminds us of the warnings we know we should heed, but don't. The author of Hebrews warns the people of God about the danger of drifting away. Words like the ones in Hebrews 2:1–3 have echoed through the centuries to all who will listen and heed them.

> We must pay the most careful attention, therefore, to what
> we have heard, so that we do not drift away. For since the
> message spoken through angels was binding, and every
> violation and disobedience received its just punishment,
> how shall we escape if we ignore so great a salvation?

Drift has claimed far too many of our spiritual siblings. Is the hypothesized apostate in Hebrews 6 one of them? Is the root of his apostasy defiance, or is there a way it could be drift sin? Is there another way to understand the "impossibility" in the text that would make drift the culprit?

Sins of Defeat

I expect we all have experienced disappointment in ourselves either for doing something we knew we shouldn't or for not doing something we knew we should do. Why can't we consistently be the person we most deeply desire to be? Why do we give in to the temptations we face every day? We succumbed to them before, realized how stupid it was to do so, then vowed to ourselves, and maybe even to God, that we never would give way to those same temptations again. Yet, we do. As we mature our sin should become less frequent, but we have all experienced the dilemma Paul names in Romans 7:18–20.

> For I have the desire to do what is good, but I cannot carry it out. For I do not do the good I want to do, but the evil I do not want to do—this I keep on doing. Now if I do what I do not want to do, it is no longer I who do it, but it is sin living in me that does it.

We are grateful God has forgiven us for past sins, but having received God's forgiveness, we still sin more than we think is reasonable for one being led by the Spirit. We cannot seem to do consistently the good we want, but we show a terrible consistency in continuing to sin. It is the classic battle of the two natures at war within us. God's Spirit gradually transforms our hearts and we grow to be more and more like Christ. But even though we become less and less entangled, we still do continue to sin.

We are disappointed, not only by our own sins, but by the sins we see in others. People we have admired, people we thought knew better. If we are short-sighted we may become critical of them for being so foolish for committing sin that should be completely absent from their lives by now. But if we take the long view, we realize that

114

everyone faces temptation, and we are not always successful in our attempts to resist it. Like Odysseus being lured by the Sirens' song, we desire the delights sin offers, but unlike Odysseus, we don't have anyone to tie us to the ship's mast. So, we succumb to their voices and sin. The Sirens win, and we are defeated.

Sins of defeat occur in the lives of Christians caught in the battle between the flesh and the spirit. Paul speaks of this battle again in Galatians 5:16–17, "So I say, walk by the Spirit, and you will not gratify the desires of the flesh. For the flesh desires what is contrary to the Spirit, and the Spirit what is contrary to the flesh. They are in conflict with each other, so that you do not do what you want." This passage should reassure people who too often find themselves on the losing side of their battles with temptation. The person in whose heart this battle is being fought desires to live righteously. The battle is evidence of that. The spiritual nature, though defeated in one skirmish, has not surrendered but is alive and striving.

If we lose too many battles, however, we begin to ask ourselves, "Why am I fighting so hard? It doesn't do any good. I still lose. Why shouldn't I just give up?" We are exhausted from fighting and weary of losing. We become so discouraged that we drop our weapons, surrender and walk slowly off the battlefield. We go AWOL. We drift away. The mistakes we make in a moment of weakness may begin to occur so frequently and consistently that our hearts lose the spirit to fight. The sins of defeat morph into the sin of drift.

Multiple defeats and the resulting discouragement, loss of fighting will, and drift, however, are not the same as defiance. Does God view apostasy the same regardless of whether it is produced by an abrupt decision to defy him, or by a gradual drift away from him? And what does the author of Hebrews mean when he says repentance is "impossible?" Is our only option to conclude that apostasy will not be forgiven, regardless of its cause? Or is the writer merely exaggerating a warning about the danger of discontinuing the spiritual battle and drifting away?

It's Impossible

How we understand Hebrews 6:4–6 and 10:26–31, especially the word "impossible," should correspond with how the original readers understood them. Our best chance to understand the book of Hebrews requires that we learn all we can about the world in which it was first written and read.

James Thompson has spent most of his academic career studying the book of Hebrews. His 2008 commentary on Hebrews explores the philosophical and linguistic backgrounds to Hebrews and illuminates our understanding of Hebrews 6.

Thompson urges us to understand Hebrews 6 in light of the rhetorical strategies common to the sermons and speeches in that time period. As Greek rhetoricians were prone to do, Thompson claims the author exaggerates the consequences of apostasy in order to persuade his readers to remain faithful. His choice to use the word "impossible" is an appeal to fear. No doubt the writer of Hebrews has a doctrine of sin, but his words in 6:4–6 are not an attempt to explain a doctrine. Rather, he employs hyperbole as a strategy to persuade his readers to remain faithful to their Christian profession. Thompson asserts that the statement, "It is impossible," is an exaggeration, and the original readers of Hebrews recognized it as such.

A simple reading of Scripture usually produces a trustworthy interpretation. Exceptions to this general rule are often due to the genre of the biblical text being studied. For example, when we read in Revelation 12 about a dragon knocking a third of the stars out of the sky by swinging his tale, we don't interpret that as an actual event. We know apocalyptic literature uses symbolism extensively. Similarly, the genre of Hebrews is homily. The writer is explicit about this when he ends his book and calls it "a word of exhortation" (13:22). Sermons include warnings and hyperbole strengthens warnings. The author of Hebrews does not intend for his remarks in 6:4–6 to be taken at face value. He is exaggerating in order to make a point.

Other biblical writers use hyperbole for emphasis. For example, John says that if everything Jesus did were written down, the whole world could not contain the resulting number of books (John 21:25). He does not mean that literally. He exaggerates as a way of emphasizing Jesus' numerous good deeds. John is not lying to his readers, because he knows they possess the capacity to recognize hyperbole.

We know how this works. Surely your mother said to you something similar to what I recall hearing from my mom: "If you don't stop antagonizing your little sister, I'm going to hang you up by your thumbs!" Mom was exaggerating. At least I think she was exaggerating. But the hyperbole in her threat got my attention in this completely hypothetical scenario regarding my little sister.

Jesus instructs us in Matthew 5:27–30 to pluck out our eyes and cut off our hands in order to keep from sinning. In a similar way, the writer of Hebrews, using the language of impossibility, wants to persuade his audience to avoid committing apostasy. Thompson's research supports this view.

> This passage is one of a series of warnings to the community about the danger that they face (cf. 2:1–4; 3:7–19). The author is neither addressing questions of church discipline nor answering questions about receiving into the community those who have lapsed during times of persecution nor addressing post-Reformation questions about the security of the believer. Indeed, the author speaks only to those who have not fallen away. Since this apostasy has not occurred, the author's words remain hypothetical.

As the frequent warnings in Hebrews indicate, (cf. 2:1–4; 3:7–4:11; 10:26–31), the concern of Hebrews is neither with church discipline nor with a theoretical discussion of the fate of apostates, for his readers have not yet fallen away. As with the warning that "they shall never enter my rest" (cf. 3:11), the author's primary concern is to awaken the listeners to the danger of abandoning God's gift.

With his use of the word "impossible" the writer of Hebrews is appropriating from his historical context commonly accepted strategies of persuasion. He is not limiting what God will or will not do. He is appealing to his readers about what they should or should not do.

> In the warning that "it is impossible again to restore to repentance," the author makes the first of four references to the impossible (cf. 6:18; 10:4; 11:6). Together with the author's consistent appeal to the "necessary" (7:12, 27; 9:16, 23) and the *fitting* (2:10), this terminology is a distinct aspect of his argument . . . . Ancient rhetorical theorists discussed the importance of the possible, the necessary, and the appropriate in deliberative argument.[2]

Is the use of the word "impossible" evidence that the apostate would be committing the unforgiveable sin? Or is Thompson's case sufficiently compelling to allow us to read Hebrews 6:4–6 as a scare tactic?

Luke 15 records the story Jesus told about the son who deliberately chose to leave his righteous upbringing and to spend a season living in wickedness. When his debauchery leads to desperation, however, his heart awakens and he repents of his excursion into sin. His father, who represents God in this story, welcomes him back

---

[2]James W. Thompson, *Hebrews*, Paideia Commentaries on the New Testament (Ada, MI: Baker Academic, 2008), 135, 124, 122.

with joy. It's a rich parable, and at least one of its messages is that God welcomes sinners who repent.

Had Benny read Luke 15 as often as he read Hebrews 6, and had he understood Hebrews 6 in its historical and literary context as Thompson's research suggests, one wonders if he could have avoided the fear and dread that plagued his last years.

Recommendations

This question as to whether those who commit apostasy can return to God's graces is not only important to the one who has fallen away. The church is also very interested in this question. First, we need to continue to develop our theology of sin, factoring in the variety of ways the Bible talks about sin and of the way God responds to each type. Second, we need to be careful not to let our interpretation of Hebrews 6:4–6 (or any other biblical passage) be determined by our desire for leniency regarding sin. The third recommendation is the flipside of the second. We have to be careful that we not heap guilt on those who have fallen away but whose hearts are genuinely remorseful for their sin. It is beyond the pale of our responsibility and authority to imply that they can never be forgiven. One way to communicate that God has forgiven them is to treat them in ways that make clear we have forgiven them. We often learn the truth about God's view of us as we see it incarnated in others' views of us. Admittedly, it is difficult to maintain the innate tension created by having high expectations that people of God avoid sin and by being generously forgiving. Nevertheless, it is a tension we must live in. Jesus' words to the woman caught in adultery are instructive: "Then neither do I condemn you," Jesus declared. "Go now and leave your life of sin" (John 8:11).

DISCUSSION QUESTIONS

1. What is the difference, if any, in the following scenarios? When should the person be forgiven? When should he or she not be forgiven?

    a. A Christian man has a single sexual encounter with a co-worker. He is grief-stricken about it, and musters the courage to tell his wife what happened, begging her forgiveness.

    b. A Christian man has an affair, and consequently leaves his wife and children. He is gone for two years, but then reappears and asks his family to forgive him.

    c. A Christian man has an affair. On his deathbed twelve years later, with full sincerity, he asks God to forgive him.

2. State in your own words the differences between sins of defiance, sins of drift, and sins of defeat.

3. A person responds to the invitation at church having been inactive in church while living a life of sensual selfishness for many years. He indicates to the shepherd who greeted him on the front row that he is truly sorry and asks the forgiveness of God and the church. You are that shepherd. Do you have any questions for the man? Would there be a follow-up conversation? If so, what would need to be discussed? What should that shepherd say to the church after having listened to the man for those three to four minutes?

4. Read Hebrews 2:1–4, 3:7–4:11, and 10:26–31.

    a. What warnings do you hear?

b. If the writer of Hebrews were in our group right now, how might he phrase his warnings to us?

5. How does the parable in Luke 15 about the runaway son affect your reading of Hebrews 6:4–6 and 10:26–31?

WHAT IS THE ETERNAL DESTINY OF THOSE WHO HAVE NEVER HEARD OF JESUS?

Danielle asks, "Jesus said, 'I am the way, the truth and the life, and no one comes to the Father except through me.' If that's true, what will happen to those people who have never had a chance to hear about Jesus? How can God be merciful and fair, yet condemn to an eternal hell those who have never had the opportunity to even hear the gospel— much less say 'yes' to it?"

lobal travel, communication technology, and multiculturalism have made us more aware than ever before of the many people who live beyond hearing range of the gospel. While it is true that the church works to take the gospel to the whole world, the reality is that it has not so far succeeded in this mission—and as far as we can tell, it will not finish this task any time soon. So, what will be the eternal destiny of those who are not Christians because they have never had an opportunity to hear the gospel, and consequently no opportunity to decide for or against Jesus?

Danielle's question challenges us to reconcile three truths that appear to be in conflict with each other: (1) Jesus claims to be the only means by which people can be saved; (2) a large percentage of the world's population either have died or will die without having heard about Jesus; and (3) many Christians believe that mercy and equity are deeply rooted in the character of God. No doubt this question is asked more today than in previous generations. To begin, let's examine each piece of this question.

First, Jesus clearly claims to be the only way to reconciliation with God when he declares, "I am the way and the truth and the life. No one comes to the Father except through me" (John 14:6). This verse alone is a sufficient foundation for what some refer to as the "radical exclusivity of Christianity." In Acts 4:12, Peter echoes this exclusive claim in one of the earliest post-resurrection declarations about Jesus: "Salvation is found in no one else, for there is no other name under heaven given to mankind by which we must be saved." Few Christians would dispute this thesis: "If you are saved, it is Jesus, and only Jesus, who saves you." However, the exclusive nature of the salvation Jesus provides is complicated by two other realities.

The second element of Danielle's question is a truth we observe about the world. A large percentage of the world's population has died without ever hearing of Jesus, and if things continue as they have in the past, millions (perhaps billions) more will also. Critics of the Christian worldview point to this reality as a main source of their cynicism. As someone disparagingly put it, "If the Bible is God's book, why did he give it to only a third of the world?"

Faced with the large number of the world's unevangelized people, some Christians counter with Jesus' words in Matthew 7:14: "Small is the gate and narrow the road that leads to life, and only a few find it." We may debate whether Jesus was referring in this teaching to final judgment or just a general truism: Only a few are willing to pay the price of discipline and hard work the good things in life require.

But what if Jesus is teaching that only a few persons in the world, relatively speaking, will spend eternity with God? If that is Jesus' meaning, then these questions follow: 1) How does one get on the narrow road? 2) Are persons confined to the road leading to destruction merely because their location in the world prohibits them from having the option to choose the narrow one? No doubt some put themselves on the broad road by spurning God's invitation to be saved. Others, however, have never received the invitation, simply because they live out of hearing range of the gospel. If these people are lost, what would that say about God's mercy and fairness?

A second way Christians try to solve the puzzle of the unevangelized is to suggest that God can be known through some form of general revelation, such as the natural world of his creation or each person's conscience. In this view, people who have not heard of Jesus still are responsible to submit to God as he has revealed himself through these means. This view is rooted, among other places, in Romans 1:18–20:

> The wrath of God is being revealed from heaven against
> all the godlessness and wickedness of people, who
> suppress the truth by their wickedness, since what may be
> known about God is plain to them, because God has made
> it plain to them. For since the creation of the world God's
> invisible qualities—his eternal power and divine nature—
> have been clearly seen, being understood from what has
> been made, so that people are without excuse.

God has chosen to reveal his power, creativity, and love of variety to all humankind through his creation. The problem, of course, is that the knowledge of God we can acquire through contemplating his creation does not by itself lead to a saving knowledge of Christ. More specific expressions of God's revelation, such as Jesus and the Bible, are required.

The third element of Danielle's question is our assumption that God is merciful and fair. We must concede, however, that one of the perks of being God is that God does not have to reconstruct himself to fit humans' ideas. On the other hand, we believe mercy lives in its truest form in God's character. God has expressed his mercy in the incarnation of Jesus and even more unmistakably in the crucifixion. God's loving kindness towards humanity is the only theological explanation for those events. Faith in God's mercy begs the question, "To what extent will God be merciful to the unevangelized?"

Christians have offered numerous solutions to the problem of the unevangelized. Each of these options is problematic, but no more so than the dilemma which they attempt to resolve. The sheer number of proposals illustrates the breadth of thinking that occurs among Christians and substantiates that intelligent and godly people can all ask a similar question, yet come away with widely divergent answers.

Options for the Destiny of the Unevangelized

Constructing a continuum will distinguish the theological options. The one below identifies eight such perspectives, each attempting to resolve the dilemma in a different way. The further you move to the left on the continuum, the more people will be included in the saved. The further to the right you move, the greater the number of people who will be excluded from the saved.

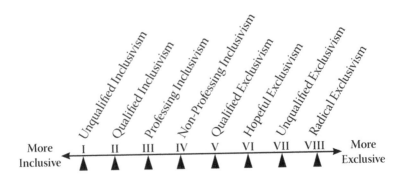

Perhaps a more accessible way to differentiate these eight views is to use the imagery supplied by Jesus in Matthew 7:13–14 of the broad and narrow roads. Using road imagery, the eight positions are distinguished as follows:

Inclusive Views

I.   There is only one road, but everyone is on it. (Unqualified Inclusivism)

II. There are many roads, and all of them lead to heaven. (Qualified Inclusivism)

III. Only the Christian road leads to heaven, but ultimately everyone will have an opportunity to get on it. (Professing Inclusivism)

IV. Only the Christian road leads to heaven, but some on the road don't know the road they are on is Christian. (Non-Professing Inclusivism)

Exclusive Views

V.   The Christian road is the only road to heaven, and to be saved we must consciously choose to get on it. But we carry on our shoulders those, like infants, who are cognitively incapable of choosing to get on the road. (Qualified Exclusivism)

VI.   The Christian road is indeed narrow, but we hope, even suspect, that somehow God may save others who are not on it. (Hopeful Exclusivism)

VII. The Christian road is indeed narrow, and God will allow only professing, obedient Christians on it. God may make exceptions to this, but we have insufficient reason to believe that he will. (Unqualified Exclusivism)

VIII. The Christian road is even narrower than most realize, and many Christians who think they are on it actually are not. (Radical Exclusivism)

Unqualified Inclusivism

Beginning on the far left, the most inclusive view is Unqualified Inclusivism. Sometimes called "universalism," this view says, "*There is only one road, but everyone is on it.*" Advocates of this perspective assert, "Surely a loving God would not condemn anyone to an eternity of torment in hell. God will save everyone in the end." They point to 2 Peter 3:9, which reveals God's desire to save everyone: "The Lord is not slow in keeping his promise. . . . Instead he is patient with you, not wanting anyone to perish, but everyone to come to repentance." Unqualified Inclusivists ask, "If God desires to save everyone, why wouldn't he? What could stop God from doing what he desires to do?"

Other Unqualified Inclusivists claim the notion of hell is untenable today. They claim the descriptions of hell, and the criteria for who will end up there, appear in the New Testament because of the unenlightened worldview that dominated the first-century world. "Even if there is a hell," they say, "God is too loving to send anyone to it. Even those who have committed the most inhumane atrocities and deserve strict punishment do not deserve an eternity of punishment more cruel than the atrocities they committed." Those who adhere to this position are convinced that every human being will be saved.

There are problems with Unqualified Inclusivism, however. First, Jesus taught that not all persons will be saved, and some will be sentenced to a place of everlasting punishment. "Anyone who says, 'You fool!' will be in danger of the fire of hell" (Matt. 5:22). To be in danger of the fire of hell presumes some could experience it. A second problem is that it undermines the necessity of Christ's atonement for humanity's sins. The Bible affirms that in order to be saved one must "call on the name of the Lord" (Acts 2:21; 22:16).

The doors of heaven cannot be propped open just because the idea of eternal punishment is distasteful.

Qualified Inclusivism

The second position on the continuum is Qualified Inclusivism. This view says, "*There are many roads, and all of them lead to heaven.*" All religious people, not just Christians, will be saved because (this view assumes) all religions have some truth in them. In his grace God draws near to everyone by whatever religion is available to them, and his mercy leads him to overlook the errors of their beliefs. After all, people can only be faithful to what they know, and this view holds that God will honor all attempts to be faithful in religious matters.

Those who hold this view (also known as "pluralism") would point to Revelation 5:9 for support: "And they [the redeemed] sang a new song, saying, 'You are worthy to take the scroll and to open its seals, because you were slain, and with your blood you purchased for God persons from every tribe and language and people and nation.'" Not every tribe of the world has heard of Jesus. That every tribe and language is represented in heaven is evidence, Qualified Inclusivists believe, that God will use many paths (including Jesus) to bring people to him. This view allows people from ethnic groups to be saved apart from hearing the Christian gospel. It also resolves the dilemma of a loving God condemning the unevangelized. Like most inclusivist views, however, it risks devaluing the exclusive "once for all" nature of Jesus' death as payment for the sins of all humanity. It further dismisses the New Testament teaching that one must have and profess faith in Christ in order to be saved. This leads to the third perspective.

Professing Inclusivism

Professing Inclusivism says, "*Only the Christian road leads to heaven, but ultimately everyone will have an opportunity to get on it.*" Proponents of this position claim that explicit knowledge of Christ is essential in order to be saved. Professing Inclusivists differ from Qualified Inclusivists primarily in that they believe that persons must confess Jesus to be their Savior in order to be saved. They point to Romans 10:9–10 as grounds for the essentiality of Christian profession:

> If you declare with your mouth, "Jesus is Lord," and believe in your heart that God raised him from the dead, you will be saved. For it is with your heart that you believe and are justified, and it is with your mouth that you profess your faith and are saved.

Professing Inclusivists further believe everyone eventually will have a chance to be saved, but for many their "saving moment" will occur through their receiving a second chance, most likely after death, to "call on the name of the Lord." They are "professing" in that they affirm faith in Jesus is essential. What makes them inclusivist is the claim that eventually God will give everyone a chance to name Jesus as Lord, though this may not occur prior to the return of Christ. Philippians 2 is a primary text for this dimension of their view:

> Therefore God exalted him to the highest place and gave him the name that is above every name, that at the name of Jesus every knee should bow, in heaven and on earth and under the earth, and every tongue acknowledge that Jesus Christ is Lord, to the glory of God the Father.

This view is inclusive and professing in that "*every* tongue will *confess*." The saved will know it is Jesus who is saving them, and they will verbally acknowledge this.

One problem with Professing Inclusivism is that Philippians 2 does not teach that those who confess Christ to be Lord when he returns will be saved. It only says that they will acknowledge him to be Lord. Persons could recognize Jesus to be Lord without placing saving faith in him as *their* Lord. The difference is important.

A second problem with this view is that if people are choosing Christ only when he returns, they may not be choosing him in faith. When Christ returns, of course everyone will recognize Jesus for who he is and call him "Lord."

When I rode the school bus in junior high, Thomas, a high school student, used to bully some of us younger riders. There is a certain way of bending and squeezing your littlest finger that is painfully persuasive. He would grab our fingers, and bend them while insisting we say something to honor him or to insult ourselves. It was a very effective method. We didn't have to *mean* what we said; we just had to say it.

If given a choice of "turn or burn," who wouldn't consent to call Jesus "Lord?" But if the "turn" is done merely for self-preservation apart from genuine faith in Christ, it would not be a legitimate conversion. A confession of Jesus as Lord upon his return could be paramount to a coerced confession rather than an authentic one.

Other advocates of this view understand the thousand-year reign of Christ described in Revelation 20 to be a literal period of time and a physical kingdom on earth. They claim that prior to the final judgment, Christ will return and reign on the earth for a millennium. During this time, everyone will learn that Jesus is indeed Lord, and will then also acknowledge him as Savior.

Professing Inclusivists claim that by some means God will give all a chance to learn of Christ. This eliminates the problem of the unevangelized, because, upon learning of Jesus, they are no longer unevangelized. It also honors the necessity of claiming Christ as the means of salvation. The problems with this view lie in the area of biblical interpretation. To be a Professing Inclusivist, one must force Philippians 2 and Revelation 20 into a particular interpretation—an interpretation driven by the assumption that God would not send anyone to hell.

Non-Professing Inclusivism

The fourth option on the continuum may be the least familiar of the views represented here. Non-Professing Inclusivism claims, *"Only the Christian road leads to heaven, but some who are on the road don't know the road they are on is Christian."* Advocates of this view believe the only way to be saved is through Jesus Christ. They also believe, however, that God will save those who live like Christians are supposed to live, even though they have never heard of Jesus. In other words, some will be included among the saved without professing faith in Jesus. This view asserts that people who love their neighbors, live righteously, serve others, and dispense mercy in all the ways Jesus desires will be counted among the saved. Sometimes referred to as "Anonymous Christians," they will be saved because they live as if they are Christians, but are "anonymous" in the sense that they are not aware that it is Christ who has saved them. In a sentence this view claims, "Everyone who will be saved will be saved through Jesus, but not everyone will know that it is Jesus who has saved them." Advocates of this view are not trying to ignore Scripture. On the contrary, they believe in the salvific, "once for all" nature of the death of Jesus taught in Hebrews 9:26–28.

> But he [Christ] has appeared once for all at the
> culmination of the ages to do away with sin by the
> sacrifice of himself. Just as people are destined to die once,
> and after that to face judgment, so Christ was sacrificed
> once to take away the sins of many.

Non-Professing Inclusivists resolve the problem of the unevange-lized by claiming the saving benefits of Jesus' death are available to those who live like Christians are called to live. The mercy of God would not categorically condemn to hell persons who demonstrate a goodness that indicates they would be Christians if they could be but, through no fault of their own, are not.

Non-Professing Inclusivists claim God will judge people on the basis of their faithfulness to the amount of divine revelation (or "light") to which their time and place in the world gives them access. God will judge people based only on what they can know, and he will not hold them responsible for what they cannot know. They find support for this view in Romans 2:12–16. There Paul says that Gentiles ("those who sin apart from the law") and Jews ("those who sin under the law") will be judged according to differing criteria.

> All who sin apart from the law will also perish apart from the law, and all who sin under the law will be judged by the law. For it is not those who hear the law who are righteous in God's sight, but it is those who obey the law who will be declared righteous. (Indeed, when Gentiles, who do not have the law, do by nature things required by the law, they are a law for themselves, even though they do not have the law. They show that the requirements of the law are written on their hearts, their consciences also bearing witness, and their thoughts sometimes accusing them and at other times even defending them.) This will take place on the day when God judges people's secrets through Jesus Christ, as my gospel declares.

The Gentiles have the general revelation of creation (Rom. 1:18–32), as well as a divinely shaped conscience (Rom. 2:15). However, Gentiles do not have the specific revelation of God's will contained in the Law. Meanwhile, the Jews have access to all of these expressions of God's revelation. Non-Professing Inclusivists see in Romans 2:12–16 a resolution to the problem of the unevangelized. They substitute "Christians" for "Jews" and "the unevangelized" for the "Gentiles." God can save non-Christians if they are faithful to the knowledge of God to which they have access.

The attraction of this view is that it honors Jesus as the only way to the Father, while discerning a way God might express his saving mercy to the unevangelized. What differentiates this view is its claim that the death of Jesus can save persons, regardless of whether they know him or not. It stops short, however, of being "universalist" (the view in which everyone is saved) because not everyone lives faithfully to the divine revelation available to them.

A primary problem with Non-Professing Inclusivism is that it includes among the saved those who have no knowledge of Jesus. Objectors acknowledge that clearly God wants all people to be saved, but equally as clear is God's requirement that people "come to a knowledge of the truth" (2 Pet. 3:9).

The Great Commission creates a second problem. Why would Jesus have commanded his followers to take the gospel to every nation if the people in those nations could be saved without hearing it? Telling the gospel to those who have never heard it puts them at risk of being condemned if they do not respond obediently to what they hear. Would it not be better for the unevangelized to remain in their ignorance of Jesus, rather than risk being condemned if they hear the gospel but do not obey it?

Other opponents of Non-Professing Inclusivism turn to Acts 17 where Paul informs the Athenians that God will not accept ignorance as an excuse.

> Therefore since we are God's offspring, we should not
> think that the divine being is like gold or silver or stone—
> an image made by human design and skill. In the past
> God overlooked such ignorance, but now he commands
> all people everywhere to repent. (Acts 17:29–30)

If God would not excuse ignorance then, what makes us think he would now?

Qualified Exclusivism

Turning now to the more exclusive options on the continuum, we come to Qualified Exclusivism. *"The Christian road is the only road to heaven, and to be saved we must consciously choose to get on it. But we carry on our shoulders those, like infants, who are cognitively incapable of choosing to get on the road."* Even those who claim that only confessing Christians will be saved exempt infants and those who are mentally incapable of believing in Jesus. I think of my friend, Luke Rusk. Born with cerebral palsy, Luke does not communicate with words, and when I look in his eyes, I am not always sure he recognizes me. Even though he is of adult age, those of us who know Luke believe he possesses a child-like mind and soul. His parents, Terry and Carol, regularly read the Bible to him. But as far as we can tell, Luke doesn't know the gospel story nor can he grasp the gospel's implications. Yet all who know Luke have no doubt he will be with us in heaven. We do not have the same expectations of Luke that we have of folks whose cognitive abilities have developed to a normal degree.

Advocates of Qualified Exclusivism make an additional exception for infants and young children for the same reason—their intellectual inability to consciously put faith in Christ and to take responsibility for their sin. God will not hold young children and the mentally handicapped accountable for sin due to the limited intellectual capacity befitting their station in life.

Other Christian tribes believe children are born innocent of sin, but that all persons reach a time in their lives when they become responsible for their own decisions and standing before God. People in my tradition call this "the age of accountability." Those who view infants as sinful, as well as those who view them as innocent of sin, share the view that, while Christianity is exclusive, there are exceptions for those intellectually incapable of Christian confession.

Non-Professing Inclusivists and Qualified Exclusivists believe God will save those who are incapable of faith in Jesus either because they lack sufficient information or intellect. Less clear is how Qualified Exclusivists respond to the problem created when the deficient ingredient is information (as is the case for the unevangelized) rather than intellect.

Before unpacking the sixth option on the continuum, it will be helpful for reasons of comparison to skip it, examine the seventh option, then return to it.

Unqualified Exclusivism

Unqualified Exclusivism affirms, *"The Christian road is indeed narrow, and God will allow only professing, obedient Christians on it. God may make exceptions to this, but we have insufficient reason to believe that he will."* There are no guarantees that anyone other than confessing Christians will be saved. The attraction of this view is that it honors the abundant biblical information that points to the necessity of a conscious dependence on Jesus as the exclusive means to salvation. The multiple conversion accounts in Acts, for example, consistently point to belief in, and baptism into, Jesus as the response whenever someone asks what to do to be saved.

An example of this will help. In Acts 16, Paul and Silas have been imprisoned for preaching and ministering in the name of Christ in the streets of Philippi. That night, chained in prison, the two were singing songs of praise to God. While they are singing an earthquake shakes the prison so vigorously that the doors fly open and the chains fall off of the prisoners. The jailer wakes to discover the opportunity the earthquake has provided the prisoners. He assumes they will have escaped, and he draws his sword in order to take his own life. We pick up the text of Acts 16 there.

But Paul shouted, "Don't harm yourself! We are all here!"
The jailer called for lights, rushed in and fell trembling
before Paul and Silas. He then brought them out and
asked, "Sirs, what must I do to be saved?" They replied,
"Believe in the Lord Jesus, and you will be saved—you and
your household." Then they spoke the word of the Lord
to him and to all the others in his house. At that hour of
the night the jailer took them and washed their wounds;
then immediately he and all his household were baptized.
The jailer brought them into his house and set a meal
before them; he was filled with joy because he had come
to believe in God—he and his whole household. (Acts
16:28–34)

In this story, Unqualified Exclusivists point out, like several others
in Acts, the jailer wants to know what he needs to do in order to
be saved. He is told there is something, and it includes believing
and being baptized. The jailer enters a saved relationship with God
through a conscious and obedient response to the gospel.

Opponents of this view object that it does not satisfactorily
deal with the massive numbers of people who, through no fault of
their own, cannot consciously choose Christ. They assert that the
claim Jesus makes to be the only way to the Father is spoken to those
who already have access to Jesus and not to those who do not have
access to him. "What kind of god," they challenge, "would condemn
people to such an extreme punishment for something over which
they have no control?" Their question is one that creates a near
insurmountable problem for many non-Christians regarding the
Christian worldview.

Others challenge Unqualified Exclusivism by claiming that
Abraham was not a confessing Christian. Living prior to Jesus made
that impossible. All Christians are confident, however, that Abraham

will be in heaven. "Doesn't that leave the door open," these challeng-ers ask, "for others living today who are not professing Christians to be saved?" The reasoning goes like this: "If Abraham and other faithful people of God who died prior to Jesus will be saved, they will be saved without having a conscious knowledge of Jesus. If they can be saved, can't we reasonably conclude that God will not be absolute in requiring a conscious profession of Jesus from people today?"

Unqualified Exclusivists respond, "We are called to preach the gospel to the whole world. The information we have prohibits our having any confidence that God will save anyone other than those who consciously follow Jesus."

Hopeful Exclusivism

We now return to the sixth point. Hopeful Exclusivism is similar to Unqualified Exclusivism but distinguishable by one factor—Hopeful Exclusivists believe God may (or will likely) save more people than Unqualified Exclusivists anticipate he will save. Hopeful Exclusivists are Qualified Exclusivists who will not be surprised to learn when they arrive in heaven that God has saved more people than most assumed. Hopefuls believe, *"The Christian road is indeed narrow, but we hope, even suspect, that God somehow may save others who are not on it."* How God will do that is beyond our knowledge, but given the nature of God's mercy and grace, they anticipate that it could happen, perhaps even that it is likely to happen.

Hopefuls look to the parable Jesus tells in Matthew 20:1–20 as evidence there may be more grace dispensed at final judgment than most assume. A vineyard owner hires workers at various times throughout the day and then at the end of the day pays them all the same wage. Those who worked all day cry "Unfair!" But the vine-yard owner replies, "What I choose to do with my money is none of your business. Why are you jealous of those to whom I choose to be exceptionally gracious?" Hopeful Exclusivists believe this parable teaches that God is prone to be more forgiving (and inclusive) in final judgment than our human sense of fairness would permit.

Radical Exclusivism

The last and most exclusive position on our continuum, Radical Exclusivism, says, *"The road to heaven is even narrower than most realize, and many Christians who think they are on it actually are not."* Radicals claim that not even all who call themselves Christians and live according to Christian morals will be saved. Only a small portion of those who claim to be Christians will be saved. They point to Jesus' words in Matthew 7:21–23 to substantiate their view:

> Not everyone who says to me, "Lord, Lord," will enter the kingdom of heaven, but only the one who does the will of my Father who is in heaven. Many will say to me on that day, "Lord, Lord, did we not prophesy in your name and in your name drive out demons and in your name perform many miracles?" Then I will tell them plainly, "I never knew you. Away from me, you evildoers!"

Jesus stuns those who seem confident of their spiritual status. "Lord, Lord," they say, but Jesus responds, "I don't know you."

Radicals contend that in addition to naming Jesus as Lord and Savior and living righteously, there are other considerations to determine who will be saved. Orthodox doctrine and church practices, for example, are additional criteria that must be considered. It is not a coincidence that every group of Christians claiming this position happens to possess unique insight as to the exact specifications of these additional criteria.

Objectors to this position argue that Radical Exclusivists do not adequately deal with the challenges their exclusivity poses to the mercy and equity of God, as well as to God's ability to make his will known to the world. Radical Exclusivists also risk requiring of believers more than the Bible explicitly requires of them, a position that tends to morph at best into an arrogant sectarianism, and at worst into a heretical legalism.

A Way Forward

There are intelligent and devout believers who have arrived at each of the positions explored above through conscientious Bible study. There are those who believe that it is inconsistent with God's mercy to think God will condemn to an eternity of torment the high percentage of the world's total population who have never heard of Jesus. There are also intelligent and sincere Christians who find in Romans 2, for example, a way God might save "anonymous Christians," the unevangelized who live as if they are Christians (morally upright, loving servants). These do not profess to be Christians, because they lack the information of the gospel to tell them how. Still others point to the numerous biblical texts that reveal God wants everyone to be saved, but to be saved they must acquire a knowledge of Jesus, confess him to be Lord, be baptized, and live as his obedient disciples. There are also Christians who hold views closer to the far right end of the spectrum. They feel they have no option but to believe the explicit teaching that there is a heaven and a hell, and that God will save only those who profess faith in Christ and faithfully adhere to a narrower set of doctrines and moral boundaries suggested in Scripture.

Which of these eight views regarding the destiny of the unevangelized is most biblically accurate? This question will not likely be resolved in the sense that one view will win over all the others. A primary frustration of not being omniscient is not being able to resolve questions of this difficulty to everyone's satisfaction. What we do know is that Jesus is the Son of God, and that he died for the sins of all people whether they are dead, living, or yet-to-be-born. We Christians have been commissioned to go and tell everyone that Jesus Christ is Lord, and to teach them to be his followers. We believe that everyone ought to know who Jesus is. Many Christians hope that more persons will be saved than any of us realize. But for others, there is insufficient biblical support for that hope.

An undisputed option we have is to obey the One who has saved us and who has commissioned us to tell the world of his great love, while trusting our heavenly Father to express his justice and mercy in a blend consistent with both.

Irresolvable questions, like that of the destiny of the unevangelized, require on-going thought, and more importantly, challenge us to listen to others' differing views with respectful humility. Questions like this one function to keep us thinking about the very important issues regarding the nature and will of God and the nature and destiny of human beings.

The desire of God is for all people to come to know Jesus. We cannot allow anything, even disputed theological issues, to keep us from working together towards that end. Meanwhile, the church needs to continue to explore questions like this one and to dialogue about them in ways that foster and preserve unity.

DISCUSSION QUESTIONS

1. With which of the eight positions does your own view most closely align?

2. Do you think responsible biblical interpretation permits us to read Romans 2:12–16 the way the advocates of Non-Professing Inclusivism read it?

3. Some have hypothesized a "geographical predestination," a view that God will give those who would respond favorably to the gospel a chance to hear it. Biblical support is drawn from Acts 17:26–27, where Paul claims that God

determines the exact times and places where people live so that they will reach out to him.

> From one man he made all the nations, that they should inhabit the whole earth; and he marked out their appointed times in history and the boundaries of their lands. God did this so that they would seek him and perhaps reach out for him and find him, though he is not far from any one of us. (Acts 17:26–27)

What do you think of this view?

4. Can you think of other biblical texts that should be considered when attempting to resolve the question of the destiny of the unevangelized?

5. Suppose you hear someone say, "I could never believe in a God who would send people to hell." What would you say to that person?

Would your response be affected by the nature of your relationship with that person? In other words, how would your response to a friend be different from your response to someone you didn't know well?

IS THE LORD'S SUPPER A TABLE OR AN ALTAR?

Alicia says, "I hear some people saying, 'The Lord's supper is a table, not an altar.' What distinction are they trying to make, and what difference would this make in our practice of communion?"

A growing practice in churches is to gather around tables and converse while eating the Lord's supper. Some think this more closely matches the practice of the early church and revitalizes today's church. Others advocate the more predominant experience of quiet reflection, and many of these are uncomfortable with, even suspicious of, the more interactive practice. Churches using both approaches are experiencing tension, and the circle of churches discussing which is most appropriate is widening. Contrasting understandings of the Lord's supper lie behind these differences and the tension.

In this chapter the word "altar" refers to an approach to the Lord's supper that focuses primarily on the cross and the forgiveness of our sins Jesus accomplished there. Approaching the Lord's supper as an altar is like observing a lamb being sacrificed as a sin offering in ancient Israel. When Christians take part in an altar experience of the Lord's supper they engage in *contemplation* and *introspection*. We remember and reflect on the death of Jesus and its saving benefits to us, and we examine our lives to see if we are living as grateful recipients of that salvation. The desired effects on us are contrition and gratitude.

In contrast, a "table" approach to the Lord's supper emphasizes the *conversation* and *interaction* between Christians as they eat it. It does not ignore the cross. Far from it. But its focus is on reconnecting with other Christians. It celebrates the cross for providing the church with its identity and mission, but believes that to primarily dwell on Jesus' death is to turn the Lord's supper into a funeral. The desired effect of "table" on Christians is increased respect for, and connection to, the other participants.

The two approaches noticeably differ from each other, and they value different activities. There are those who advocate a more interactive, communal experience of the Lord's supper. They claim, "We remember the death of Christ in the supper just like everyone else, but remembering doesn't have to be done in somber silence. And, after all, the Lord's supper is a celebration, and in no other setting would you see celebration done silently. No one would dare go to a birthday party and sit in a corner and contemplate. When we attend a birthday party we celebrate the honoree's birth, and celebration is evident in the laughter and high-spirited interaction."

On the other hand, those who advocate a more contemplative, solo experience might respond to the "interactives" by saying, "But when we eat the Lord's supper we are not attending a birthday party. We are honoring a life and remembering a death, much like we do at funerals. Birthday parties and communion require different kinds of remembering. The difference between the Lord's supper and a funeral is that Jesus rose from the dead. So any sadness that is present during our quiet reflection is due to our sorrow in thinking that it was our sins that put Jesus on the cross. We also believe the Lord's supper is a celebration. We just believe that to practice the supper like you do would be so distracting that it would eventually lose its connection to the cross. It could become merely a party. In our silent reflection, we are merely remembering what Jesus did for us on the cross. Just like the Jews would not have thought about eating the Passover without remembering the Exodus, so Christians cannot eat the Lord's supper without remembering the death of Jesus."

Those who prefer the more interactive experience might counter, "We accept that in the supper you are honoring the Lord, but maybe you should consider using some other phrase than 'celebrating the Lord's supper' to describe communion as you practice it. No real celebration is as somber as what we observe in you."

To Contemplate or to Interact?

When using the terms table and altar many are no doubt referring to John Mark Hicks's book, *Come to the Table.* Hicks argues that the practice of the Lord's supper by modern Christians has emphasized a more individualistic experience, whereas Scripture calls us to a more communal meal like the ones enjoyed by the earliest Christians. A few representative statements from Hicks summarize his view:

> Our practice of the supper as a silent, solemn, individualistic eating of bread and drinking of wine is radically dissimilar from the joyous communal meal that united Christians in first-century house churches.

> Altar is the dominant model for the supper in the contemporary church. . . . To revision the supper as "table" will foster community, interactive communion, gratitude, and joy.

> The Lord's supper is never described as an "altar" in Scripture. Instead, Paul explicitly dubs it "the Lord's table"

(1 Corinthians 10:21). Indeed the table/altar distinction is rooted in the Hebrew sacrificial ritual. The blood is shed and poured at the altar, but the animal is eaten at the table. The cross is the Christian altar, but the Lord's supper is its table. The two are connected as those who eat at the table participate in the benefits of the altar, but the two are distinct. The altar is a place where the guilty bring their sins for atonement, but the table is where the forgiven experience communion with God. The altar is a place of death and sorrow, but the table is a place of hope (life) and joy. The believer seeks reconciliation at the altar, but experiences reconciliation at the table.... The Lord's supper is a meal eaten at a table. It is not a sacrifice offered at an altar. Understanding this fundamental difference will reshape the practice of the supper in the contemporary church.[3]

In other words, Hicks claims we have taken communion without being very communal.

Is Hicks correct in his assessment of the nature of the Lord's supper and how it should be practiced? Is the biblical evidence for a table view strong enough to support his call for a revisioning of the Lord's supper? If so, what implications would this have for our contemporary practice of it? And, especially given the aim of this book, how could such a revisioning foster maturity in us rather than animosity between us?

---

[3] John Mark Hicks, *Come to the Table: Revisioning the Lord's Supper* (Abilene, TX, Leafwood Publishers, 2002), 9–10, 10, 185–186. See also Hicks, *Enter the Water, Come to the Table: Baptism and Lord's Supper in the Bible's Story of New Creation* (Abilene: Abilene Christian University Press, 2014).

Remembering, Celebrating, Interacting

As the Gospels of Matthew, Mark, and Luke indicate, the supper eaten by Jesus and his disciples on the night of his arrest was a Passover celebration. Rooted in the experience of the Israelites in Egypt and the Exodus, the Passover meal was a commemoration and celebration of God's deliverance of his people from the grip of Pharaoh. Participants remember and celebrate their new identity as a freed people. The memory of their deliverance prompts the celebration. The memory provides the meaning to the meal. Celebrating without remembering would be like blowing out candles on a cake but not acknowledging anyone's birthday.

The Passover is both predecessor to the Lord's supper and also a parallel to it, inasmuch as both contain the elements of memory, celebration, and interaction. Perhaps the tension between the altar and table approaches is a result of eating the Lord's supper while neglecting one or more of the activities of remembering, celebrating, or interacting.

The Passover meal is the predecessor to the Christian practice of the Lord's supper. As Jesus eats the Passover with the disciples, he takes the bread and wine and invests them with new meaning. It is as if Jesus is saying, "From now on, do this in memory of *me* (not the Exodus). Just as God delivered the Israelites through Moses, God will deliver you through me." True, the last supper was eaten by a community around a table. But Jesus also gave it an altar emphasis when he instructed the disciples to remember him and the blood he would soon shed. Matthew 26:26–29 records the scene in these words:

> While they were eating, Jesus took bread, and when he
> had given thanks, he broke it and gave it to his disciples,
> saying, "Take and eat; this is my body." Then he took a cup,
> and when he had given thanks, he gave it to them, saying,
> "Drink from it, all of you. This is my blood of the covenant,

> which is poured out for many for the forgiveness of sins.
> I tell you, I will not drink from this fruit of the vine from
> now on until that day when I drink it new with you in my
> Father's kingdom."

Discussions attempting to discern whether the Lord's supper is more *altar* or *table* must deal with the emphasis Jesus placed here on his death. Perhaps we should understand the instructions of Jesus to remember him as support for the altar view. Table advocates might challenge this and say, "It's fine to remember Jesus, but it seems to us that Christians too often partake of the Lord's supper as if they are renewing their forgiveness, like we renew our vehicle registration."

John's account of the last supper provides a different perspective on the last supper of Jesus and the twelve. We will explore John 13 later in the chapter.

Altar and Table at Corinth

Paul's treatment of the Lord's supper in 1 Corinthians 11:17–34 is the most extensive in the New Testament. It is not surprising to see elements of both table and altar approaches in his corrective instructions. The church in Corinth is riddled with problems, and Paul reveals that the assemblies of the Corinthian church are counter-productive and characterized by division.

> In the following directives I have no praise for you, for
> your meetings do more harm than good. In the first place,
> I hear that when you come together as a church, there are
> divisions among you, and to some extent I believe it. No
> doubt there have to be differences among you to show
> which of you have God's approval. (1 Cor. 11:17–19)

Their assemblies are more damaging than constructive. The divisiveness addressed early in the letter (1 Cor. 1:10–15; 3:1–5) has now surfaced in their assemblies. The sarcasm present in Paul's statement, "No doubt there have to be differences among you to show which of you have God's approval," is designed to dispel the ridiculous notion that one group is superior to the others. Paul next scolds them for isolating themselves and excluding others from their tables.

> When you come together, it is not the Lord's Supper you
> eat, for when you are eating, some of you go ahead with
> your own private suppers. As a result, one person remains
> hungry and another gets drunk. Don't you have homes
> to eat and drink in? Or do you despise the church of God
> by humiliating those who have nothing? What shall I say
> to you? Shall I praise you? Certainly not in this matter!
> (1 Cor. 11:20–22)

Even though they are consuming bread and wine, their fractured community disqualifies the meal from being the Lord's supper. This is a classic example of the distinction between a practice's form and its meaning. One can be immersed in water without undergoing the transformation baptism symbolizes. One can wear a wedding ring but not fulfill the vows for which the ring is a seal and reminder. Likewise, the meal shared by the Christian community is not primarily about ingesting food. Paul is saying, "If you come here merely to satisfy your hunger, you can do that at home. That's not what *this* meal is about." We can ingest the forms of bread and wine while in the same room and still fail to manifest the inclusive community into which Jesus calls us.

Paul accuses the Corinthians of despising the church of God by eating their bread and wine in isolation from others. He attempts to reset their understanding and practice by reviewing the last supper Jesus had with his disciples.

> For I received from the Lord what I also passed on
> to you: The Lord Jesus, on the night he was betrayed,
> took bread, and when he had given thanks, he broke it
> and said, "This is my body, which is for you; do this in
> remembrance of me." In the same way, after supper he
> took the cup, saying, "This cup is the new covenant in my
> blood; do this, whenever you drink it, in remembrance of
> me." For whenever you eat this bread and drink this cup,
> you proclaim the Lord's death until he comes. So then,
> whoever eats the bread or drinks the cup of the Lord in
> an unworthy manner will be guilty of sinning against the
> body and blood of the Lord. (1 Cor. 11:23–27)

Here Paul identifies the variety of activities that should occur as we take the Lord's supper. First, the supper is a time of reflection, inasmuch as we remember and contemplate the death of Jesus. It is also an experience through which we announce the death of Jesus. More specifically, we claim and proclaim the atoning significance of his death. While looking back to his crucifixion, we anticipate Christ's return "until he comes."

Paul names other activities that should characterize our meal. "Everyone ought to examine themselves before they eat of the bread and drink from the cup. For those who eat and drink without discerning the body of Christ eat and drink judgment on themselves" (1 Cor. 11:28–29). As we eat, we examine ourselves and discern the body of Christ. Are we discerning the physical body of Jesus as it hung on the cross or the spiritual body of Jesus, the church? It could be both, but the context indicates it most certainly includes the latter. Perhaps Paul intends for the ambiguous language to make it difficult to separate the two.

Paul also highlights the inseparable connection between healthy, loving interaction with other Christians and individual spiritual health. He says, "That is why many among you are weak and sick, and a number of you have fallen asleep" (1 Cor. 11:30). Christians become weak and sick when divisions sabotage community.

Paul concludes by insisting that their meal become more interactive, or more table-like.

> So then, my brothers and sisters, when you gather to eat, you should all eat together. Anyone who is hungry should eat something at home, so that when you meet together it may not result in judgment. And when I come I will give further directions. (1 Cor. 11:33–34)

Paul insists that this meal does not become communion (literally, "with union") if the other Christians present are treated as if they were invisible.

Two statements summarize Paul's instructions in 1 Corinthians 11:17–34. First, "You are not the community you are called to be unless you derive your identity from the self-sacrificing Savior." This is the act of remembering. Second, "You are not eating the Lord's supper until it becomes an experience of community." This points to the activities of celebrating and interacting.

Where in the Bible do we find images of community that could inform our practice of communion? Paul frequently used the human body to describe our relationships and attitudes to each other. We exercise our gifts in the body of Christ in a variety of ways: we serve each other (Rom. 12:3–8), we rejoice and weep with each other (Rom. 12:15), we recognize the importance of every member (1 Cor. 12:12–27), and we help each other mature in Christ (Eph. 4:11–16). The New Testament also offers images of family (Gal. 6:10), royal priesthood (1 Peter 2:5), and a holy nation (1 Peter 2:9). There are other images as well.

Living Between Eden and Jerusalem

Parker Palmer, a prolific writer in the field of education, identifies three additional biblical images for community.[4] Genesis 1–2 describes a perfect garden. In Eden there is harmony, peace, and fellowship in their purest forms. There, humans walk with God. Their nakedness symbolizes their radical vulnerability, yet they are unashamed. They have not yet been tarnished by sin or humiliated by pride-driven, dehumanizing comparisons. What heart doesn't yearn for such an experience of healthy community?

The second image Palmer identifies is that of a city, in particular, the one described in Revelation 21. Descending from heaven, the New Jerusalem is, like Eden, perfect. No sin. No sorrow. There are no tears, because there is nothing to cry about.

> I saw the Holy City, the new Jerusalem, coming down
> out of heaven from God, prepared as a bride beautifully
> dressed for her husband. And I heard a loud voice from
> the throne saying, "Look! God's dwelling place is now
> among the people, and he will dwell with them. They will
> be his people, and God himself will be with them and be
> their God. 'He will wipe every tear from their eyes. There
> will be no more death' or mourning or crying or pain, for
> the old order of things has passed away." (Rev. 21:2–4)

In this holy, heavenly city, everything is wonderful. There is no pain, no death, no mourning, and no crying. We are living with God in his home, and he is gently comforting us by wiping away the tears from our past trials. The holiness permeating this city prohibits any of the demoralizing, life-destroying realities we experience now. Like Eden,

---

[4] Parker J. Palmer, "On Staying at the Table: A Spirituality of Community," in *Introduction to Faith, Reason and Justice, Custom Reader, Eastern University: INST 150, 2005–2006* (Littleton, MA: Tapestry Press, 2005), 77–81.

this city-to-come resonates deeply with the longing of our hearts for a community of *shalom.*

Palmer claims, however, that Eden and Jerusalem are presently unusable by us as images for community. They both lie outside history, untouched by the present human experience of sin. The perfect garden existed prior to sin's entrance, and sin's exit will not occur until the arrival of the heavenly city. Meanwhile, we're stuck here—with each other. Our present experience of community is laced with disappointment, self-protectionism, loneliness, cynicism, and other relationship-destroying maladies. A bleak contrast to Eden and Jerusalem, our experience reminds us of the old slogan, "To dwell above with the saints we love, that will be grace and glory. But to dwell below with the saints we know, well, that's another story."

What we need is an image of community that fits our experience of living between the garden and heaven, between humanity's perfect beginning and its perfect end. Palmer claims we need an image of an imperfect community living in a sin-infested world. He finds that image in a table.

Table is a fitting image for the church, because the seats around the table are filled, as in our families, with fallible people—people who will disappoint, exclude, rage and enrage, criticize, and sin in ways unbefitting those who should know better. We welcome the sense of belonging and support family provides, but our experience also includes conflict, hurt feelings, and the fatigue that comes from caring and burden-bearing. The table shared by Jesus and his disciples is similar to our tables. John 13 transports us to that table where we witness the kind of imperfect community with which we are too familiar.

Wash and Come to the Table

Jesus is with the twelve to eat the Passover meal, fully aware of all that is about to happen. Jesus knows Judas will betray him, that Peter will deny him, and that everyone seated around this table will soon abandon him. In a few minutes, Judas will leave under the guise of running an errand on behalf of the group. But Jesus knows exactly where he's going. And if the conversation around the table that night was anything like some of the disciples' previous exchanges, there were arguments, competitive bragging, jockeying for position, desires for status and the power that accompanies recognition, and multiple other expressions of self-centeredness. Hardly a band of brothers.

Even knowing these things, Jesus stands up, gets a towel and a basin of water, and begins to wash the feet of all those present—Judas, Peter, the other ten. All 120 toes. But Peter resists this gesture.

> He came to Simon Peter, who said to him, "Lord, are you going to wash my feet?" Jesus replied, "You do not realize now what I am doing, but later you will understand." "No," said Peter, "you shall never wash my feet." Jesus answered, "Unless I wash you, you have no part with me." "Then, Lord," Simon Peter replied, "not just my feet but my hands and my head as well!" Jesus answered, "Those who have had a bath need only to wash their feet; their whole body is clean. And you are clean, though not every one of you." For he knew who was going to betray him, and that was why he said not every one was clean. (John 13:6–11)

Jesus washes the feet of the disciples much like his blood washes our souls. The emphasis in John's account of the last supper is not on remembering, though it being a Passover meal, they surely would have done that. Here the emphasis is on cleansing. Jesus washed the people at table with him, then instructs them to love and serve each other (John 13:15–17).

We also, like the original disciples, are "already clean" having been washed in our baptism. Around the table, we re-embrace our need for his continuing cleansing by permitting Jesus to wash our feet. Those who advocate that we eat the Lord's supper in silence have a point. In our reflecting we re-connect with the forgiveness provided to us through Jesus' death. Others say our experience of the Lord's supper needs to be more interactive, allowing us to re-connect with each other much like a family would do at the dinner table. So where do altar and table meet?

John 13 makes it clear that cleansing is a necessary prerequisite to communing. When Peter resists, Jesus insists, "Unless I wash you, you have no part with me." The cleansing was made possible by the cross. In our reflection we remember that Jesus has bathed our souls in his blood. Christians in the Middle Ages were taught (incorrectly) that they weren't forgiven until they ate the Eucharist. But we do not gain access to Christ's forgiveness by eating the Lord's supper. We gain access through our faith. And being clean is what we celebrate. Peter resists having his feet washed, claiming he needs a whole bath. Jesus tells him and us, "You are already clean." We just need our feet washed. We just need refreshing, like a restaurant server might periodically return to our tables to replenish our beverages. Eating the supper we remember that we have been cleansed, and in our remembering, it is as if we are being washed afresh.

Being washed is a prerequisite to staying at Jesus' table. As we eat the Lord's supper we "proclaim his death" and the cleansing it performs. On the cross, Jesus ran the bath water. When we were baptized, we entered the water and were cleansed. Forgiveness is the skin we live in on a daily basis. When we eat Lord's supper we remember the source of our cleansing. Having been cleansed from the impurities that divide us, we turn to love and serve each other as Jesus taught all his disciples to do. In this way, remembering, celebrating, and interacting are all present.

Around the table with Jesus were sinful persons, just as there are around the table we gather around each Sunday in our congregations. But we are not surprised. Judas and Peter with their betrayal and cowardice are present at our table as well. The same community eroding dynamics present at the last supper are among us. All the ingredients are present to produce cynicism and disillusionment.

So what do we do? We commit to stay "at table," that's what. We don't bail with Judas, sharing his selfish disillusionment. Instead, we remain seated, compassionately engaged, humbled by our own spiritual inconsistencies, and mesmerized by our host. In a sense we are always at table with the church, but especially so when we assemble on the Lord's Day to eat the supper together. At the supper of Jesus, the main course is forgiveness—the forgiveness Jesus offers to us and the forgiveness that we extend to the others seated with us. This is where the Lord's supper as altar intersects with the Lord's supper as table. We form our community around the cross. Calvary is both the dinner bell that calls us to the table as well as its centerpiece. And as a centerpiece the cross is not there to decorate the table, but to define it.

At an earlier moment in his ministry we find Jesus again at table, this time in the home of Matthew the tax collector (Matt. 9:9–12). There, Jesus is surrounded by a variety of sinners, and the Pharisees disapprove of his choice to be at table with folks like that. What the Pharisees do not realize is that "folks like that" are the only kind of folks there are. When we gather around the Lord's table, Matthew and all his friends are there with us. They feel comfortable at table with us, because, like them, we also have come not only to "say grace" but to consume grace and pass it to others.

I remember clearly the auditorium where I grew up attending church. A communion table sat at the front, directly underneath the pulpit. (I enjoy thinking about how our furniture arrangements manifest our values.) The table's material and design matched the pulpit and pews. I was baptized at age eleven a few feet from that table. Even now I can smell our blue songbooks, feel the back of the pew in my hands as we stood to sing, and be transported in my memory to what was for me a sacred space.

In the side of the table facing the congregation were inscribed the words, "Do This in Remembrance of Me." Even though we sat in the pews while the bread and "the fruit of the vine" (as we were careful to call it) were served, we were still metaphorically gathered around a table. Looking back, however, I don't think we realized it. Forty years ago the question as to whether the Lord's supper is a table or an altar was not in our consciousness. The Lord's supper was a weekly experience through which we remembered that Jesus died for our sins and without him we would be lost. The remembering softened our hearts to God and often to each other, and made us grateful. The only table present in our experience of the supper was the wooden one that held the trays of bread and juice.

Is it an altar or a table we gather around when we eat the Lord's supper? The older I get, the more wary I am whenever I see questions cast in a way that assumes an either-or answer. Many times the best answer is more of the both-and variety. Perhaps the way forward in this conversation is not "altar *or* table," but "altar *on* table." This both-and option embraces both the sacrificial and the communal dimensions of the supper. It combines the contemplation and introspection of 1 Corinthians 11:27 with the conversation and interaction alluded to in 11:33–34. While our theology may permit a blend of the two approaches, our practice may take a little longer.

One of the strengths of my heritage in the American Restoration Movement is its insistence on eating the Lord's supper every Sunday. We combine Acts 20:7 with 1 Corinthians 16:1–2 and conclude that the early Christians also did so. We are also intent to partake of it correctly. Since "correctly" must always be defined by the Bible, we must continually shine the light of Scripture on our present understandings and practices. Continued study will help ensure that our practice is guided more by Scripture than by our desires for comfort or for innovation.

Paul's insistence that the Corinthian Christians experience the Lord's supper in ways that foster inclusion and interaction certainly challenges those of us practiced primarily in the art of altar. As we submit our familiar practices to the light of God's Word, however, two truths become clear. Our altar needs altering, and our table needs the cross as its centerpiece. Each approach could benefit from what the other values. Blending the two approaches will no doubt call us to be more creative, and may even require that we rearrange the furniture from time to time.

Recommendations

The recommendations offered here assume that most Christian churches practice the Lord's supper as more of an altar than as a table. Some find it easier to move from a practice of the supper as table to one of altar, than from an altar model to one of table. The task becomes how to move towards a more table-like experience of the Lord's supper without alienating those who believe the supper is more an altar and who are uncomfortable with the more interactive approach. Wouldn't it be disappointingly ironic if, by coercing our brothers and sisters to practice the Lord's supper as a table, our attempts to foster community actually produced alienation instead? We would be committing our own version of the Corinthians' error.

Implementing a more balanced experience of the Lord's supper will no doubt require considerable creativity. Experimenting with some practices will aid us in developing more and more helpful ways to put the community back into the communion. Here, I offer only a few ideas.

First, when introducing the Lord's supper, the presider can pose questions or offer ideas for reflection and discussion. Some examples may help:

1. Presider: "As you pass the bread to the person next to you, say to him or her, 'This is the body of Christ. We are the body of Christ.'"
2. Presider: "We are about to take the Lord's supper. As you pass the bread and wine to the next person, turn to him or her and say, 'Christ loved us so much that he died for us. Let's learn to love each other that much.'"
3. Presider: "As you eat the bread, say to the person next to you, 'Jesus lived a perfect life. Let's try to follow his example.'"
4. Presider: "In a moment, I am going to ask you to stand and turn to someone near you. Each of you is invited to express your response, and listen to your neighbor's response to this question: 'As we think of Peter denying that he knows Jesus, can you tell of a time when you are most tempted to deny your association with Jesus?'"
5. Presider: "As you drink the wine, say to a person near you, 'This represents the blood which Jesus shed and which forgives us our sins. If I have done anything unloving to you, I ask you to forgive me also.'"

Second, we can literally place tables around the meeting room and invite people to join (or take) others there to eat the Lord's supper together. My church does this. Our members are given the option of getting up and going to a table to eat the supper or to remain seated and be served. Some really enjoy going to the table, while others are uncomfortable doing so. Many prefer to remain seated and sit in silent contemplation, a practice that frustrates some of the rest of our members.

On a recent Sunday morning as the servers began to pass the bread and fruit of the vine, I spotted a man and his son four rows in front of me. The two had just recently lost Alex, their daughter and sister. I knew I should invite them to go with me to the table, but my feet seemed to be stuck to the carpet. Unless preaching or teaching, I do not like everyone to be looking at me, and I knew the moment I got up that's what would happen. Finally, I mustered Golden Rule courage, got up, and approached them. Fortunately, they were seated next to the aisle. I leaned over and asked, "Would you both join me at the table?" Their facial expressions signaled they were eager to do so, and thankful to be asked. We went to a small table in the back. As we ate the supper, I said to them, "I know you still miss Alex. I just wanted you to remember that we all love you." They both thanked me, the dad with tears in his eyes. The point of this anecdote is to illustrate how we might practice a more communal experience of communion. Buy some tables.

Third, you can create interactive communion experiences more easily with a smaller group where it is easier to mingle and talk. So, if you are a part of a Christian small group, create a time to commune in a more interactive way. You may discover a practical idea you could share with the larger church.

Finally, let's share our ideas and create new ones. A practical way to do this in your church is to convene a team of individuals to identify creative ways to lead your church in more balanced experiences of remembering, celebrating, and interacting. Be sure to include people who prefer the more contemplative approach and those who prefer the more interactive approach. (The committee ought to be a microcosm of the church reflecting both its diversity and its unity.) Obviously, the church's leadership would need to be on board. No one likes to be ambushed.

The desired outcome of these recommendations is, of course, for the people of God to gain a stronger attachment to Jesus and to each other, and for the world to take notice and say, "Clearly, God is among them."

DISCUSSION QUESTIONS

1. Tell of your memory of first witnessing or of eating the Lord's supper.

2. What do you think about John Mark Hicks's characterization that in many churches the Lord's supper is more about silence and solemnity than it is an expression of community? Is his assessment accurate?

3. Do you think it matters whether or not a church's practice of the Lord's supper has a balanced mix of memory, celebration, and interaction? What blessings are forfeited if one is present and another is absent?

4. Are you more familiar with experiencing the Lord's supper as table or as altar?

5. Practically speaking, how can we experience the Lord's supper in ways that honor both its altar and its table dimensions?

6. Whichever approach your church is most accustomed to, what ideas do you have about how the Lord's supper could be experienced as a better blend of table and altar?

7. Jesus tells a parable recorded in Luke 12:35–40 about a homeowner who returns from a trip to find his servants ready for him. They have acted loyally and responsibly while he's been away. Verse 37 says that the master will be so pleased that he will dress himself to serve and will have his servants recline at table. Then he will wait on them.

   Do you think it is a legitimate interpretation of this parable to think Jesus might be referring to himself as the host?

In other words, is Jesus suggesting that our experience of heaven will be like our sitting at a banquet table at which Jesus is both host and butler? If so, what might that imply about our practice of the Lord's supper now as a dress rehearsal for that banquet?

DO WE WORSHIP ON SUNDAY OR EVERY DAY?

Tony reports, "The preacher at our church says, 'Worship is not what we do on Sundays when we are at the church building; worship is what we do 24/7.' I know our daily lives are to reflect that we are God's people, but I am concerned that he is minimizing the importance of the Sunday assembly. What does the Bible really say about worship?"

Tony's question reveals two differing points of view regarding worship. We can call the first one "the assembly view" and the other one "the daily view." The differences between the two are substantial and potentially divisive. On the one hand, those who emphasize the assembly view of worship are concerned we not minimize the central place of the Christian assembly in the life of the church. Attending church helps keep Christians connected to God as well as to each other. In that sense the assembly is like a family reunion in which you renew ties with cousins with whom you would likely lose connection were it not for the contact the reunion provides. We can all agree that the current trend of decreasing church attendance is alarming.

On the other hand, there are those who advocate that worship is something that occurs primarily in our daily living. Though the Christian assembly is certainly one setting in which we express our worship, the daily view claims that to think our worship occurs chiefly in the Christian assembly can lead to our devaluing how we live for Christ in our homes, neighborhoods, and workplaces. To be fair, neither side is totally one or the other. The daily view believes worship occurs in the assembly, and the assembly view affirms our daily living as a form of worship. The difference is a matter of degree and primary emphasis.

There are at least three significant consequences at stake in this discussion. First is a perspective of the Christian life. Does our faith integrate every hour of every day equally, or is there a sense in which Sunday morning takes on a heightened importance to God and therefore to us? A second consequence is the criteria by which we identify the people of God. Is righteous living the hallmark of Christianity or must Christians conduct their assemblies in particular ways in order to be counted among the faithful? A third potential consequence is linked to the importance placed on the Christian assembly. What if the church never met together? Could it continue to be the church?

To understand these two views of worship, we must first discuss the origins of "worship as assembly" and then examine the biblical teachings regarding Christian worship. This chapter will conclude with recommendations for a practice of worship that embraces the truth contained in each view.

Roots of the "Worship as Assembly" View

The modern concept of "the worship service" as a Sunday gathering of Christians can be traced partly to the historical context of early Christianity (in the first through third centuries) and partly to the practices of medieval Christianity. As the earliest Christian churches came into existence, most of the Greco-Roman world worshipped pagan deities in huge and ornate temples of marble. But these colossal structures were not only places of worship; they were also thought to be the dwelling places of the gods or at least of their material likenesses. To pagans, these temples were sacred places, but Christians increasingly disdained these temples as the implications of idolatry became clearer.

Jewish Christians living in the Jerusalem area in 40 or 50 AD would have likely continued their worship in the temple, at least until Christianity came to be viewed as a separate entity from Judaism rather than a sect within it. Outside of Jerusalem, however, Jewish Christians did not have daily access to their temple. Gentile Christians were very familiar with conducting worship in a temple, since temples dominated the landscape of ancient Greece and Rome. But conducting worship in a pagan temple was not an option for early Christians given their aversion to idolatry and the fact that they didn't have one of their own. Instead, they met in homes. In other words, all the evidence suggests that early Christians intentionally avoided pagan temples, sometimes worshipped in the Jewish temple, but mainly assembled for worship in each other's homes.

Modern Christians don't consciously think of their church buildings as temples. They embrace the Bible's teaching that God dwells in the church and in the lives of individual Christians. The New Testament teaches that God's people are his temple. Paul declared that individual Christians are temples of the Holy Spirit (1 Cor. 6:18–20), and Peter affirmed that Christians together make up a temple of worship (1 Pet. 2:4–5). The daily view, on the other hand, assumes that Paul and Peter use temple imagery because they are introducing a totally new way of understanding worship: in this view, Christian worship is intentionally de-centralized, de-institutional-ized, and de-compartmentalized. The assembly view affirms that the people of God comprise the temple of God, but they also assert that the assembly is still the primary place where worship occurs, even if it is conducted in a plainly decorated building.

Our modern views of worship are shaped not only by early Christianity, but also by the practices of the medieval church. Medieval Christianity, due in part to a resurgence of interest in Greek philosophy, practiced a temple-centered approach in the form of Christian cathedrals. Housing sacred icons of the medieval church, European cathedrals became sacred spaces. Before Johannes Gutenberg made copies of Bibles more prevalent, most medieval Christians, usually illiterate anyway, had no direct access to the Bible's stories. Instead, they learned the stories of scripture from the sculptures, paintings, and iconography that filled medieval and (later) Renaissance cathedrals. These works of art were not used primarily for decoration, but rather for the education of common Christians and the veneration of God, Christ, and the various saints the works of art represented. While there was good in this visual strategy—to be fair, more good than is sometimes admitted—one consequence of the cathedral's function as the center of spiritual formation and worship was a reinforced sense that worship takes place primarily in a temple-like structure.

The rise of monasticism throughout the middle ages could be interpreted in part as a reaction to, if not an effort to counteract, the dominant cathedral-centered approach. Monastics sought to show through their dedicated living and practices that their entire lives were devoted to God. However successful monasticism was in posing an alternative to cathedral-centered Christianity, it did not replace it. So, unlike the early church, medieval Christianity, just as in the ancient pagan and Jewish contexts, conducted the activity of worship in a central location.

It's easy to see how we Christians in the twenty-first century are still affected by the medieval cathedral-centered concept of worship. Despite multiple attempts at reform, the idea of "worship" being something we do when we gather in a physical structure (a cathedral or chapel, or church building, or auditorium), an inherently holy space, is deeply engrained in the Christian mind, and it has changed little as the centuries have passed. In Christian congregations today one can get the distinct impression that we believe there is something sacred about our church buildings. We have a latent sense that the space itself is part of what makes our worship holy. Our theology is more sophisticated than this, but our practices say differently.

I remember as a child wearing a collared shirt, freshly polished shoes, a clip-on tie, and a jacket to church. I also recall brother Bob, an older member of our church, regularly leading a song from where he sat just a few minutes before the assembly was scheduled to begin. Almost always his choice of hymns consisted of these lyrics: "The Lord is in his holy temple. Let all the earth keep silence before him. Keep silence. Keep silence. Keep silence before him." This brother was reflecting a widely held understanding that when we assembled we were somehow more in the presence of God than otherwise. Our practice of wearing our "Sunday best" clothes supported this view.

Sunday Mornings

Almost all Christian traditions place a high priority on the Sunday Christian assembly, and many of these define their identity by the specific forms of worship that occur within it. For these Christians, carrying out the right activities in the right way has been a crucial mark of authentic Christian identity. In the tradition to which I belong, these activities are often referred to as "acts of worship." They include 1) the weekly observation of the Lord's supper, 2) reading and preaching the Word, 3) singing songs of praise and exhortation, 4) weekly collection of financial contributions to support the ministries of the church, and 5) public prayer. We have attempted to conduct these activities in ways that imitate the practices of the earliest Christian churches. Like numerous other Christian traditions, we frequently have referred to this Sunday assembly as "the worship service." In the worship service, reverence for God is fostered and expected. That reverence tends to extend to the acts performed during worship in the assembly. What's more, we tend to discuss these acts of worship with language that links them to ancient temple ritual. Singing becomes "a sacrifice" of praise; the collection of money given to sustain the church's ministries is sometimes referred to as "the offering." The correspondence between temple concepts and our own practices of worship is indeed high.

The recent introduction of the catch-phrase "worship is 24/7" marks a reaction against the long-standing, temple or church-building centered views of worship. A growing number of Christians have come to believe through Bible study that the worship described by the Bible embraces more than just the Sunday assembly. The daily view affirms that Sunday morning assembly of Christians is indeed important, but not only because of the assembly's worship. It tends to assume that worship goes on seamlessly throughout a Christian's life, individually during the week and corporately in the assembly. The assembly is important, but for reasons of mutual encouragement more than as an occasion for worship.

To those with a long experience of equating worship with the Christian assembly, this downplaying of the importance of worship in the assembly can feel disorienting, even threatening. It certainly poses several implications for Christian understandings and practice. If a church's identity is tied to how the assembly is conducted, attempts to recast its function or its importance will pose a threat. On the other hand, imagine how empowering it would be if Christians truly thought of their daily lives as the primary way they worship God.

Thankfully, the Bible does not ask us to choose between meeting together on Sundays or living righteously, though both activities could be enriched and energized by what the Bible says about each. If we as Christians are committed to look to the Bible as authoritative in matters of life and faith, we must examine our ideas and practices, including our notions of worship, alongside biblical teaching.

Worship and the Christian Assembly

Those emphasizing the importance of worship in the assembly are right to do so. Hebrews 10:24–25 links assembly participation as both a cause and an effect of Christian faithfulness: "And let us consider how we may spur one another on toward love and good deeds, not giving up meeting together, as some are in the habit of doing, but encouraging one another—and all the more as you see the Day approaching." The daily view of worship points out that this text makes explicit that the purpose of the Christian assembly is for Christians to encourage each other. Nothing is said here to lead us to conclude the assembly is about worship.

The assembly view, on the other hand, counters by saying that the verses immediately preceding these borrow extensively on the activities of the high priest in the temple, thus connecting our assemblies to a temple-like experience:

> Therefore, brothers and sisters, since we have confidence to enter the Most Holy Place by the blood of Jesus, by a new and living way opened for us through the curtain, that is, his body, and since we have a great priest over the house of God, let us draw near to God with a sincere heart and with the full assurance that faith brings, having our hearts sprinkled to cleanse us from a guilty conscience and having our bodies washed with pure water. Let us hold unswervingly to the hope we profess, for he who promised is faithful. (Heb. 10:19–23)

Thus, while the assembly's explicit purpose in Hebrews 10 is mutual encouragement (not worship, explicitly), the assembly is also tied by the temple-like functions of drawing near to God and being sprinkled and washed.

To make matters more complicated, though, while Hebrews 10 does discuss worship in Old Testament temple terms, we must remember that the Old Testament itself often emphasizes faithfulness in daily life over temple worship. In Psalm 51, for example, David says that God will not delight in his sacrifices until his heart has been cleansed from infidelity. Likewise, the Old Testament prophets weighed daily living more heavily than worship in the temple. Their temple worship was often unacceptable because the people were not living righteously. Isaiah 1 is representative of numerous similar passages:

> "The multitude of your sacrifices—what are they to me?" says the LORD. "I have more than enough of burnt offerings, of rams and the fat of fattened animals; I have no pleasure in the blood of bulls and lambs and goats. When you come to appear before me, who has asked this of you, this trampling of my courts? Stop bringing meaningless offerings! Your incense is detestable to me. New Moons, Sabbaths and convocations—I cannot bear your worthless assemblies. Your New Moon feasts and your appointed festivals I hate with all my being. They have become a burden to me; I am weary of bearing them. When you spread out your hands in prayer, I hide my eyes from you; even when you offer many prayers, I am not listening. Your hands are full of blood! Wash and make yourselves clean. Take your evil deeds out of my sight; stop doing wrong. Learn to do right; seek justice. Defend the oppressed. Take up the cause of the fatherless; plead the case of the widow." (Isa. 1:11–17)

Wherever Christians worship today, it is clear that the people of God are called to righteous living and godly character, and no amount of worship done in a building can supplant that.

New Testament Vocabulary for Worship

A careful examination of the six Greek words used in the New Testament to refer to worship reveals that worship, as the New Testament writers understood it, is not something confined to one holy day or holy location. The six words related to worship in the New Testament are *threskeia* and *sebomai* (both meaning "to worship"), *proskuneo* ("to prostrate oneself before"), *leitourgia* and *latreuo* (both meaning "to perform a religious service"), and *eusebia* (in different contexts meaning "piety," "godliness," or "religion"). Outside of the Bible these words *did* refer to temple worship as they were used, in Greco-Roman and Jewish culture at large. However, the New Testament writers infused these words with new and very different meanings. Below, examples from Hebrews 12–13, 1 Peter 2, James 1, and Romans 12 will illustrate how Christian writers broadened their meanings in some creative and inspiring ways.

Throughout the New Testament, *proskuneo, leitourgia, latreuo, threskeia, sebomai,* and *eusebia* seldom if ever refer to the Christian assembly, but rather to the way Christians are to live at all times. As Everett Ferguson, retired professor of early Christian writings and backgrounds at Abilene Christian University, explains,

> These [Greek] words for worship derive from the ritual actions of the Greco-Roman world, especially the temple service, both pagan and Jewish. Notice, however, what Christianity has done to these words. Instead of referring to ritual or ceremonial activities, the language of cult [temple ceremonies] is applied to the Christian life, especially its moral conduct and good deeds.... Not

> only do the words of worship in the ancient world not
> refer in their Christian context to ritual or cultic acts,
> but rarely do they occur even in regard to the Christian
> assembly. . . . Consequently, any distinction in principle
> between assembly for worship and service in the world is
> ruled out . . .[5]

In other words, the evidence we can gather from the New Testament
writers' vocabulary is decidedly one-sided: it consistently supports
the daily view of worship. As the next sections of this chapter will
show, the New Testament does *not* use these words to refer to the
gathering of Christians on Sunday. The one possible exception may
be Acts 13:1–3:

> Now in the church at Antioch there were prophets
> and teachers: Barnabas, Simeon called Niger, Lucius of
> Cyrene, Manaen (who had been brought up with Herod
> the tetrarch) and Saul. While they were worshiping the
> Lord and fasting, the Holy Spirit said, "Set apart for me
> Barnabas and Saul for the work to which I have called
> them." So after they had fasted and prayed, they placed
> their hands on them and sent them off.

"While they were worshipping the Lord . . . the Holy Spirit said . . ,"
certainly sounds like the worship could be referring to an assembly context. On the other hand, the mention of fasting indicates
the "worshipping and fasting" may be referring to a more extended
period of time, since fasting is an exercise that consumes more time
than an assembly requires. Regardless of the meaning of "worship"
in Acts 13, all other references to worship in the New Testament
using any of these six words represent worship as a daily offering

---

[5] Everett Ferguson, *The Church of Christ: A Biblical Ecclesiology for Today*
(Grand Rapids: Eerdmans, 1997), 211.

of our selves rather than as the "acts of worship" associated with a Christian assembly.

Some may be wondering, "What difference does it make?" The difference is significant, and after exploring some of the New Testament texts regarding worship, we will explore some of the implications of this profound shift from pre-Christian understandings of worship to Christian ones.

Hebrews 12–13

The daily view points to two texts in Hebrews 12–13 as evidence that the Christian concept of worship leaves behind the idea of "worship as assembly" in favor of "worship as daily living." Chapter twelve ends with a beautiful statement about God and our worship of him: "Therefore, since we are receiving a kingdom that cannot be shaken, let us be thankful, and so worship God acceptably with reverence and awe, for our God is a consuming fire" (Heb. 12:28–29). The daily view claims that this command to worship God that ends chapter twelve is logically connected to chapter thirteen's opening list of specific ways to worship:

> Keep on loving one another as brothers and sisters. Do
> not forget to show hospitality to strangers, for by so doing
> some people have shown hospitality to angels without
> knowing it. Continue to remember those in prison as if
> you were together with them in prison, and those who are
> mistreated as if you yourselves were suffering. Marriage
> should be honored by all, and the marriage bed kept
> pure, for God will judge the adulterer and all the sexually
> immoral. Keep your lives free from the love of money and
> be content with what you have . . . . (Heb. 13:1–5)

Those who claim worship is daily point out that for the original readers, and for centuries afterwards, no chapter number separated the text of 12:29 and 13:1. Their point is that with no break between what are our chapters twelve and thirteen, this text expresses a powerful insight. We worship God in reverence and awe, and we worship him *by* our faithful actions in daily life. We worship by loving, by showing hospitality, by ministering to prisoners, by protecting the sacred nature of our marriage covenants, and by being content rather than materialistic.

Those who hold to an assembly-centered view of worship are quick to point out that earlier in the same chapter the writer said, "But you have come to Mount Zion, to the city of the living God, the heavenly Jerusalem. You have come to thousands upon thousands of angels in joyful assembly" (Heb. 12:22). It seems clear in the assembly view that the admonition to worship God in reverence and awe is mentioned in the same context as the reference to the joyful assembly in heaven. Worship in Hebrews 12 is done in an assembly.

Perhaps the most balanced interpretation would see Hebrews 12 as depicting worship *in community.* Along these lines, chapter thirteen goes on to use language of worship that points to both the assembly and to daily living. Our sacrifices include the praise from our lips as well as our good deeds: "Through Jesus, therefore, let us continually offer to God a sacrifice of praise—the fruit of lips that confess his name. And do not forget to do good and to share with others, for with such sacrifices God is pleased" (Heb. 13:15–16).

1 Peter 2

Peter's words in this text establish the principle of the "priesthood of all believers" which has meant so much to Christians across the centuries. "As you come to him, the living Stone—rejected by humans but chosen by God and precious to him—you also, like living stones, are being built into a spiritual house to be a holy priesthood, offering spiritual sacrifices acceptable to God through Jesus Christ" (1 Pet. 2:4–5). Here Peter is retooling "temple" imagery. In ancient Israel, holiness depended on three necessary ingredients: the priest, the temple and a sacrifice. Jesus embodies these in his own life. As we follow Christ, Peter claims, Christians are now simultaneously the temple (a spiritual house), the priests (a holy priesthood), and the sacrifices (spiritual sacrifices). This passage sums up ideas emphasized by a number of other scriptures: Jesus claims in John 2 that his body is the temple, and the book of Hebrews emphasizes his role as our high priest (Heb. 7:1–8:6) and as the ultimate sacrifice for our sins (Heb. 9:11–28). 1 Peter 2:4–5 is valuable for our understanding of worship because it (1) shifts the locus of worship from a place (the temple) to a people (all Christians), (2) empowers all Christians by designating them to be priests, and (3) calls us to sacrificial living. Like Hebrews 12:28–13:16, 1 Peter 2:4–5 implies that Christians' faithful actions in daily life define their identity. These "worship" passages do not directly address the Sunday assembly at all, but the clarity of their commands about "faithful worship" in daily life suggests that it is what Christians do throughout the week, above and beyond the details of their Sunday assembly, that defines their authenticity and identity in God's sight.

Practically speaking, if we Christians are the priests, the temple, and the sacrifices, no matter where we are, all the ingredients are present for "the holy" to emerge. A temple built by humans is not necessary for worship to occur, nor does worship primarily occur in church gatherings.

Romans 12

Paul's command to "offer your bodies as a living sacrifice" at the beginning of Romans 12 is the pivot on which the book's argument turns, and it offers a crucial insight about worship. Romans can be divided into two major parts: a descriptive section, followed by a prescriptive one. The descriptive section describes what God has done through Christ for his people; the prescriptive section prescribes how we should act in response to what God has done. In Romans, chapters 1–11 describe how God has expressed his mercy to both Jews and Gentiles. Chapters 12–16 prescribe how that mercy should transform Christians' lives. The first part of the book explains how we are saved; the second part gives us instructions about how we should live. Romans 12:1–2, with its link between God's mercy and Christians' transformed living, is the hinge between the two sections.

> Therefore, I urge you, brothers and sisters, in view of God's mercy, to offer your bodies as a living sacrifice, holy and pleasing to God—this is your true and proper worship. Do not conform to the pattern of this world, but be transformed by the renewing of your mind. Then you will be able to test and approve what God's will is—his good, pleasing and perfect will. (Rom. 12:1–2)

All of the instructions that Paul will give in chapters 12–16 are prefaced by this statement that offering our bodies as *living* sacrifices—not offering slaughtered animals as sacrifices—is, for us Christians, "true and proper worship." It is a revolutionary idea, given the dead Jewish and Greek temple sacrifices continually being offered as Paul wrote this letter. Romans 12:1–2 signals a complete transformation. Worship is no longer a ritual confined to the temple, but all of daily life lived for God. The sacrifices are no longer animals, but our selves. Most importantly, the sacrifices are not dead, but living. In fact, living is necessary for the worship to occur, as God's will engulfs every part of his people's lives and his power works through them to reconcile and redeem and transform the world. But we Christians have to re-decide every day to put ourselves on the sacrificial altar. "The problem with living sacrifices," beloved missions professor Wendell Broom used to say, "is that they tend to want to crawl off the altar."

In the verses and chapters that follow, Paul goes on to detail exactly what this transformation should look like throughout every facet of Christians' lives. *When we think of sacrifice not only as something we do, but as something we are, we worship God on a continual basis.* Whether the worship is acceptable depends on whether our hearts, our conduct and our treatment of each other manifest that Christ lives in us.

James 1

In one of the New Testament's most concise statements on what God expects of his people, James says: "Religion that God our Father accepts as pure and faultless is this: to look after orphans and widows in their distress and to keep oneself from being polluted by the world" (James 1:27). The word translated "religion" here is the word *threskeia,* one of the six Greek "worship" words mentioned above. Outside of the New Testament *threskeia* is used to refer to cultic rituals, the kind that would be carried out in a pagan temple. Here James teaches the profound truth that our religion is not performed in a temple at a specified time, but through the mercy we dispense to others and the degree to which we live in holiness. Ministry and holiness cannot be limited to specific times or places. They are character traits that deep-dye our lives.

It should be clear how James's "pure and faultless" religion lines up with the other apostles' explanations of worship discussed above. Just as Paul transformed the meaning of "sacrifice" in Romans 12, James here redefines temple-worship as the way Christians live day-to-day in a broken world.

Those advocating worship as daily activity claim the biblical evidence is clear: the New Testament intentionally and decisively shifts the meaning of "worship" *away* from something that is done periodically at a specially designated place and time—something Jewish and Greek converts would have taken for granted—and makes "worship" engulf the whole of Christians' daily lives. If we are serious about our claim to let the Bible be our guide in faith and practice, the daily view insists, Scripture calls us to adjust our understanding and practice of worship today.

This is not to say the assembly is unimportant. It only says that the assembly is important for reasons other than the primary locale of our worship. To compare our current practice with the teachings of the New Testament, the assembly is less important to our worship than we have thought, and our daily living is more important to our worship than we have thought.

The following recommendations can help us correct our course towards a genuine New Testament theology of worship.

Implications and Recommendations

First, let's think of worship more holistically than we have done in the past. The temptation to segment our lives is understandable. We fill many roles in our lives. We are siblings, spouses, parents, children, employees, neighbors, church members, and community volunteers. When I am on the job, I am acting as a teacher, and even though in reality I am also a husband and father, no amount of multi-tasking can eliminate the basic reality that, practically speaking, I function in one role at a time. That inescapable compartmentalization of our roles tempts us to compartmentalize our worship to a specific time (Sunday morning) and place (the church's building). A more holistic, integrated view of worship, however, requires us to change our thinking. Some think of their roles as slices of a pizza, and our worship of God is just one slice of the pizza sitting alongside the other functions of our lives. A more holistic way of thinking about our lives, and

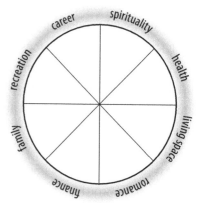

about worship, is to think of our faith and our worship as the entire crust on which sit all our roles and pursuits. The activities and roles are merely toppings; our worship is the crust.

Thinking holistically, we must recognize that our worship of God cannot be confined to the Sunday morning assembly at the church building, or to any other single place or time. We are worshiping every day in every action. While we may not feel we are worshipping every moment of every day, our praise is the character we possess and display, and our praying is manifested through daily action. I like the way Allison, a former student, said it: "Your life becomes the prayer."

Second, let us resolve to use vocabulary that reflects biblical, rather than pagan, notions of worship. There is much wisdom in the commitment to use biblical words to represent biblical ideas. In the question that started this chapter, when Tony's preacher advocated a "24/7" view of worship, he was calling for a more biblical way of talking about worship. Correcting our language so that "worship" is no longer equated (and thus limited to) the assembly could go a long way toward correcting the tendency to compartmentalize one's faith and worship. Since the New Testament does not use "worship" to refer to the Sunday assembly, let's not do so either.

So how should we talk about our Sunday assemblies? Some might advocate that we use the phrases "corporate worship" to refer to the assembly and "individual worship" to refer to our daily lives as sacrifices. Alternatively, we could use the phrase "the Christian assembly" to refer to our Sunday gatherings and "Christian living" to refer to the godly and generous living advocated and spoken of in the New Testament as "worship." If the New Testament does not refer to the Sunday assembly as worship, why should we? Doing so compartmentalizes our worship into one portion of our lives rather than the whole of our lives. As my colleague, Kevin Youngblood, puts it, "Worship is recognizing that (and behaving as if) God is the center of the universe." We gather each Sunday with others who affirm that God is the center of the universe. This recognition intensifies when we are gathered with others who also recognize it, and perhaps that is why our assemblies can feel more like worship than other times of our week.

Third, and most important, if Christian worship is indeed an all-encompassing way of living, even daily activities such as studying, working, and interacting with others become primary means of worship. The activities that occupy such a large percentage of our days take on an increased significance because they are ways of expressing our gratitude and praise to God. *The worship that the New Testament prescribes breathes God's kingdom into every minute of our days and sanctifies every action of our busy lives.* Imagine how much the mission of God in the world would benefit from Christians who lived as if their daily righteousness was the primary way to manifest devotion to God.

The biblical texts that address the duties of Christian slaves speak most directly to our conduct in day-to-day work. Paul gave the following instructions to the Christian slaves in Colossae:

> Slaves, obey your earthly masters in everything; and do it, not only when their eye is on you and to curry their favor, but with sincerity of heart and reverence for the Lord. Whatever you do, work at it with all your heart, as working for the Lord, not for human masters, since you know that you will receive an inheritance from the Lord as a reward. It is the Lord Christ you are serving. (Col. 3:22–24)

Working, caring, serving, befriending, playing, relaxing, struggling— whatever we do becomes worship if it is done as a service to Christ. Grateful recipients of his mercy, we attend the Christian assembly each week because it is there that we re-embrace our identity as children of God and encourage each other to live faithful to our profession. We leave the assembly ready to do what we can, through our daily living and working, to contribute to his mission in our world. Our living becomes a prayer and our serving a song of praise.

DISCUSSION QUESTIONS

1. Prior to reading the Scriptures in this chapter, what was your understanding of the purpose of the Christian assembly?

2. What is your view now? Where in the Bible do you find support for your view?

3. What do you imagine would be the effect of changing our language from "worship is what we do on Sunday in the assembly" to "worship is everything we do every day?"

4. How is the Christian assembly similar to and different from the following analogies?

    - A football team in a huddle
    - A pile of coals
    - A 12-step group
    - A ship's crew

5. What difference might it make if we were to think of the following activities as worship to God?

    - School work
    - Singing praises
    - Duties associated with employment
    - Household chores (taking out the trash, washing the dishes, cutting the lawn)

TOWARDS PEACEFUL AND PRODUCTIVE DIALOGUE

We were in the fifth grade, as I recall. It was just after Wednesday night Bible class in what we called "the annex," a white wooden house our church had purchased and re-located next to our building for additional classroom space. My friend Melody and I started arguing about what the letters AD in historical dates stood for. We both agreed BC was an abbreviation for "Before Christ." Looking back, I am embarrassed to admit that I was advocating that AD stood for "After Death." Somehow I had gotten it into my head that if one abbreviation included the word "before" then the other naturally would have to include the word "after." (Don't laugh too loud; even Wikipedia, that unquestionable source of public knowledge, confirms this is a common mistake.) I never convinced Melody to switch her view to mine. She insisted that the abbreviation was Latin for *Anno Domini*, "in the year of our Lord." (That was circa 1968. The option of whipping out a smart phone and Googling the answer was not available to us.) She was right, of course. I was wrong, even though I remained adamant that I wasn't. Mostly, I was miffed that a girl my age knew Latin. I remember two things about that argument: we didn't resolve it that night, and I left frustrated and unclear as to what should happen next.

Looking back, a more humble and productive response would have been: "I've always thought AD meant 'after death.' Why do you think it means *Anno Domini*? Let's go look it up in a dictionary together. Maybe I am mistaken." I admit that would have been a pretty mature response for an eleven-year-old. But it's not out of reach for us adults.

This book has sought to examine controversial issues to help us discuss them without dividing over them. It is important to remember, here at the end, that discussing them openly may not necessarily resolve them. Many issues that interest and plague us cannot be resolved. But the more achievable and equally important goal is to conduct our discussions in ways that foster unity. In Ephesians 4:3, Paul tells us, "Make every effort to keep the unity of the Spirit through the bond of peace." He tells us *how* to do so in the preceding verse: "Be completely humble and gentle; be patient, bearing with one another in love" (Eph. 4:2–3).

How well we treat each other before, while, and after we discuss controversial questions may be even more important than arriving at a working solution. *The process is as important as the product.*

Fruitful dialogue about controversial topics is rare because, among other things, it requires intense listening. There never seems to be enough listening going on in any setting, from international relations to Congress to our churches to our homes. In conversations we tend to talk rather than attempting to understand what others are saying. And since today's phone technology allows us to carry the internet in our pockets, it is common to see a room full of friends allowing their phones to distract them from really listening to each other.

When I was in grad school, I took a course in Christian counseling. On the first day, the professor announced, "In this class we are only going to do one thing. We are going to learn how to listen." I remember punching the guy next to me and saying, "This is great.

I already know how to do that." But I didn't. Still, I learned; and I can say definitively that no skill has been more helpful in my relationships and in my ministry than attentive listening. I don't always listen as well as I should, but now I know how, if I just will. We can acquire additional listening skills, but to listen effectively to each other the most important factor is our will—a desire to understand each other.

I once heard Greg Taylor talk about the Golden Commission—fulfilling the Great Commission according to the Golden Rule. "Teach the Gospel to others the way you would want them to teach it to you." I like that.

I want to call us to *Golden Disagreements*. Let's disagree with others the way we would want others to disagree with us. We would want others who disagree with us to be terrific listeners, to assume the best regarding our intentions, to respect our intellect, and to ask us why we think the issue is important.

The sum of everything I've learned so far about discussing controversial questions with others, and staying Christ-like while doing it, comes down to two principles. First, heed biblical wisdom. Second, heed the wisdom of experience.

These two brief lists of suggestions can help to nurture peaceful and productive dialogue. If our conversations are to foster and preserve unity, we must pay careful attention to how we conduct them. Scripture and experience both teach us that if the conversation isn't peaceful, it doesn't stand much of a chance of being productive.

Biblical Wisdom for Peaceful and Productive Dialogue

1. Be the first one in the conversation to assume the role of listener. "Be quick to listen, and slow to speak" (James 1:19-20). "To answer without listening is folly and shame" (Prov. 18:13).

2. Practice the Golden Rule as you talk. If we translated Matthew 7:12 with conversation specifically in mind, it would read like this: "In every conversation, listen and speak to others the way that you would want them to listen and speak to you."

3. After you have listened well, and it's time for you to make your case, cast everything you say in gentleness and respect. "But in your hearts revere Christ as Lord. Always be prepared to give an answer to everyone who asks you to give the reason for the hope that you have. But do this with gentleness and respect" (1 Pet. 3:15). Treating others with respect helps conversations be more peaceful and more productive, but it would be the right thing to do even if it didn't.

4. Speak the truth lovingly or don't speak at all. "Instead, speaking the truth in love, we will grow to become in every respect the mature body of him who is the head, that is, Christ" (Eph. 4:15). A loving tone and demeanor is the spoonful of sugar that helps us swallow medicinal truth.

5. Is the conversation getting heated? Need to calm someone down? Use kind words and demeanor. Find something you can sincerely affirm in the other person. "A gentle answer turns away wrath, but a harsh word stirs up anger" (Prov. 15:1).

6. Hold on to humility. Most of the Christians I know already possess a general spirit of humility. But even those who ordinarily are humble may permit themselves to set humility aside when discussing controversial issues. Granted, it is not easy to hold deep convictions and still not come across as a "know-it-all." But we need what scholars call an "epistemological humility." That's university-speak for being humble regarding what I know and the ways in which I

186

came to know it. It is to be open to the possibility that I am wrong or that my viewpoint needs to be modified.

Wisdom from Experience for Peaceful and Productive Dialogue

1. Seek first to understand, then to be understood. Many will recognize this as one of Stephen Covey's "Seven Habits of Highly Effective People." I have consistently found that if I will take the time to understand the other person's viewpoint, I always get a listening ear for mine in return.

2. Avoid saying, "I understand." Assume you do not understand. Ask this question: "Let me see if I understand you correctly. Are you saying _____ ?" And keep asking it until you receive an unqualified "yes" in response. It is the other person's place to tell you if they feel you have understood them. Communication has not occurred until the sender acknowledges that the receiver has understood both the content of the message and the feelings of the sender.

3. Read about active, empathic listening. Start here and follow some of the helpful links this one contains: http://www.colorado.edu/conflict/peace/treatment/activel.htm.

4. Active, empathic listening is a skill you can acquire and strengthen. Practice it. Listen carefully to learn others' values and fears—what they think is important and what they are afraid will happen. When it comes to getting your point across to another person, listening often contributes as much as speaking.

5. Listen to their eyes as well as their words. Their eyes are the windows of their heart. If you focus intently on their eyes as you listen, it will enable you to better understand what

other persons are trying to say to you, as well as how they are responding to what you are saying to them.

6. Be fully present. Give one hundred percent of our attention to the person in front of you. Randy Harris has said, "The best gift you give another person is your undivided attention." He's right. So keep your eyes on theirs and your phone in your pocket.

7. Give people the benefit of the doubt. People tend to be smarter and better than we sometimes give them credit for.

8. Be authentic and non-manipulative. Say what you mean, and don't talk to others with hidden motives. No one responds well to manipulation.

9. Risk vulnerability. Take twenty minutes to view Brené Brown's TED talk "The Power of Vulnerability." If we want to connect deeply with others, and if we want them to understand us, we will have to risk being vulnerable.

10. Accept that good reasons don't always succeed in persuading. Some resist reason as if to say, "My mind's made up; don't confuse me with the facts." Reason has its place, but many times people choose their views based more on what makes them comfortable than on what is reasonable. People may be adamant in their opinions because they fear the discomfort that would come if they adopted a different view. When familiar tradition and unfamiliar truth collide, people will usually choose the comfort of what they presently know and do. If they don't seem to be accepting your views, try to identify the discomfort that would come to them if they did so.

11. In your attempts to lead others to understand and accept your point of view, don't attempt to intimidate or pressure them. You cannot force people to change their minds. You can only offer them alternative perspectives and reasons

for embracing them. An elder in Memphis once offered to me this wisdom: "People can change, but they will not *be* changed."

12. Imagine how you would want the person to report to others your conduct during the conversation. Conduct yourself in ways that allow your behavior in the conversation to be spoken of in this way: "Even though I still disagree with him, we had a healthy conversation. I would enjoy talking about this with him again."

13. Give up the goal of winning the argument and win a friend instead. (If the discussion becomes an argument, chances are no one will end up really winning anything worth having.) Instead, seek to use the conversation to build a friendship. Keep the door open for future conversations.

◆   ◆   ◆

My good friend Brant Bryan says, "We are nothing if we are not people of hope." He's right. Let's keep hope alive. Let's keep pursuing unity and peaceful dialogue, no matter how far out of reach they may seem. May this book, in some small way, strengthen your hope that the diversity of opinions we see around us will, in the end, build up the body of Christ. May we explore the tough questions we face with peacefulness and respect, and may God restore our unity.

FOR FURTHER READING

The following titles provide a deeper understanding of how different Christians approach the questions this book has addressed. These suggested readings are representative rather than exhaustive, and no attempt is made here to steer readers to the "right" answers. The suggested readings below serve only to give you a beach from which to "wade into" the discussions (past and present) about these questions.

Chapter 1
Why Is There So Little Unity among Christians?

Differing interpretations of the biblical text pose one of the greater challenges to Christian unity. Robert K. Johnston explores the dilemma of interpretation in *Evangelicals at an Impasse: Biblical Authority in Practice* (Atlanta: John Knox, 1979). N. T. Wright, who is being widely read today on many topics, contributes some refreshing insights on biblical interpretation and authority in his *Scripture and the Authority of God: How to Read the Bible Today* (New York: HarperCollins, 2011). For a concise expression of some of his ideas, see the transcript of his lecture found at http://ntwrightpage.com/Wright_Bible_Authoritative.htm or Rachel Held Evans' accessible overview of five of Wright's recommendations for reading Scripture found at http://rachelheldevans.com/blog/wright-5-recommendations-scripture.

The tone we use when we discuss our differences is another significant challenge to unity. Our demeanor may say more than our words. Studies on communication, especially those exploring "emotional intelligence" and "emotional competency" can help us grow in our abilities to communicate more productively. (Emotional incompetence, by contrast, would be the inability to see how anger and poor listening skills undermine communication.) Leland R. Beaumont has collected some helpful resources on emotional competency at http://www.emotionalcompetency.com. Likewise, Harold Heie provides a guide to peaceful dialogue in *Learning to Listen, Ready to Talk: A Pilgrimage Toward Peacemaking* (Lincoln, NE: iUniverse, 2007). Heie also offers a model of peaceful dialogue between Christians in *Evangelicals on Public Policy Issues: Sustaining a Respectful Political Conversation* (Abilene, TX: ACU Press, 2014).

Chapter 2
How Should We View Christ Followers in Other Christian Traditions?

Obviously the questions of unity (Chapter 1) and of how to view others who live in the name of Christ are linked. Some have found the conversations about "bounded set" and "centered set" models to be helpful here. See Tim Harmon's brief yet helpful introduction to "set" thinking at http://www.westernseminary.edu/transformed-blog/2014/01/17/whos-in-and-whos-out-christianity-and-bounded-sets-vs-centered-sets/, or Brian McLaren's discussion in *More Ready Than You Realize* (Nashville: Zondervan, 2002). McLaren names four kinds of thinking related to "set" theory: Bounded, Centered, Process, and Journey.

James Woodroof examines this question for those in the heritage of Churches of Christ in *The Church in Transition* (Searcy, Ark.: Bible House, 1990). F. LaGard Smith, in *Who is My Brother? Facing a Crisis of Identity and Fellowship* (Nashville: Cotswold Publishing, 1997), names five levels of fellowship: Universal, Faith, In Christ, Conscience, and Congregational. Rubel Shelley casts a persuasive vision for undenominational Christianity in *I Just Want to Be a Christian* (Nashville, Tennessee: 20th Century Christian, 1984). The book includes some of the more influential documents, like "The Last Will and Testament of the Springfield Presbytery," that shaped the American Restoration Movement. Monroe Hawley makes a similar appeal for a Christian basis for unity in *Re-digging the Wells* (Abilene, Texas: Quality Publications, 1976).

Chapter 3
How Should the Church Face the Issues Surrounding Homosexuality?

Robert Gagnon's *The Bible and Homosexual Practice: Texts and Hermeneutics* (Nashville, TN: Abingdon Press, 2001) provides an admirably thorough analysis of the biblical texts related to homosexuality. Further resources are grouped here according to the four facets of the question explored in Chapter 3:

How should the church respond to Christians who practice homosexuality?

Everett Ferguson offers an informative introductory treatment of church discipline on pages 373–389 of his book *The Church of Christ: A Biblical Ecclesiology for Today* (Eerdmans, 1997).

How should the church respond to Christians struggling with same-sex attraction?

There is a growing field of thought on this question. Mark Yarhouse rejects homosexual activity as sin while identifying many aspects of homosexual practice as social constructions. In his book *Homosexuality and the Christian: A Guide for Parents, Churches and Friends* (Bloomington, MN: Bethany House, 2010), Yarhouse recognizes three types of homosexual experience: same-sex attraction, homosexual orientation (long-term same-sex attraction accepted as a personal norm), and gay identity (a cultural construction of self and group identification). While Yarhouse claims that one may experience "same sex attraction" independent of homosexual behavior, homosexual orientation and gay identity require a cognitive acquiescence. For a contrasting perspective, see Matthew Vines, "The Gay Debate: The Bible and Homosexuality" at http://www.youtube.com/watch?v=ezQjNJUSraY. A gay Christian, Vines claims we have misinterpreted the biblical passages that address homosexuality. Regarding possible factors behind same-sex attraction in males, see http://genderwholeness.com/lds/understanding/what-causes-male-homosexuality/. Autobiographical accounts by Christians with same sex attraction help us better understand the dilemmas they face. See Sally Gary, *Loves God, Likes Girls: A Memoir* (Abilene, TX: Leafwood, 2013); Mel White, *Stranger at the Gate: To Be Gay and Christian in America* (New York: Plume, 1995); and Wesley Hill, *Washed and Waiting: Reflections on Christian Faithfulness and Homosexuality* (Grand Rapids, MI: Zondervan. 2010).

How should the church respond to non-Christian homosexuals?

Andrew Marin's *Love Is an Orientation: Elevating the Conversation with the Gay Community* (Downers Grove, IL: InterVarsity, 2009) is a useful guide for churches in ministering to the gay community. Jenell Williams Paris argues in *The End of Sexual Identity: Why Sex Is Too Important to Define Who We Are* (Downers Grove, IL: InterVarsity, 2011) that the Christian response to homosexuality should not be to "defend heterosexuality," but to look past and rise above the divisive and unbiblical identities of "gay" and "straight."

How should the church respond to the cultural trend to legalize homosexual unions and legitimize homosexuality as a lifestyle?

The church's relationship to culture in general and to government more specifically is a discussion containing numerous components and little consensus. Should Christians try to shape public policies and, if so, which ones, and how should we go about doing so? Two books provide a starting place for exploring these questions. One is named above in the readings suggested for Chapter 1: Harold Heie, *Evangelicals on Public Policy Issues: Sustaining a Respectful Political Conversation* (Abilene: ACU Press, 2014). The other is Ronald J. Sider and Diane Knippers, eds., *Toward an Evangelical Public Policy: Political Strategies for the Health of the Nation* (Grand Rapids, Michigan: Baker Books, 2005). The latter attempts to deepen evangelicals' understanding of political involvement and to unify and strengthen the evangelical presence in politics. Those affiliated with Churches of Christ may be interested in the *Christian Chronicle's* editorial of March 2014 and the responses it generated: http://www.christianchronicle.org/article/a-christian-response-to-anti-gay-laws.

Chapter 4
Can Women Lead the Christian Assembly?

On the debate over women in leadership in the larger evangelical world, see James R. Beck and Craig L. Blomberg, eds., *Two Views on Women in Ministry* (Grand Rapids: Zondervan, 2001), as well as Thomas R. Schreiner's helpful review of this volume in the *Journal for Biblical Manhood and Womanhood* (http://www.sbts.edu/documents/tschreiner/6.2_review.pdf). A volume edited by Ronald W. Pierce and Rebecca Merrill Groothuis, *Discovering Biblical Equality: Complementarity without Hierarchy* (Downers Grove, IL: Intervarsity, 2005) contains 29 articles by more than 20 evangelical contributors. The articles are grouped in five sections:

Setting the Stage (the Historical Backdrop), Looking to Scripture (the Biblical Texts), Thinking It Through (Logical and Theological Perspectives), Addressing the Issues (Hermeneutical and Cultural Perspectives), and Living It Out (Practical Applications). Craig S. Keener treats the pertinent New Testament texts in *Paul, Women & Wives: Marriage and Women's Ministry in the Letters of Paul* (Peabody, MA: Hendrickson, 1992). Scot McKnight's *The Blue Parakeet: Rethinking How You Read the Bible* (Grand Rapids, MI: Zondervan, 2008) probes the issue of women in ministry as a test case in biblical hermeneutics. McKnight argues for an egalitarian practice which he calls "mutualism." McKnight's book is critiqued by James White in his review entitled "The Hidden Agenda of the Blue Parakeet," which may be found at http://www.equip.org/articles/the-hidden-agenda-of-the-blue-parakeet/#christian-books-5.

For perspectives of members within Churches of Christ, Carroll D. Osburn offers an excellent overview of this discussion in *Women in the Church: Reclaiming the Ideal* (Abilene, TX: Abilene Christian University Press, 2001). Less restrictive positions are explored in Sara Barton's *A Woman Called: Piecing Together the Ministry Puzzle* (Abilene, TX: Leafwood Publishers, 2012). The website at http://gal328.org/ exists "to promote gender justice in the Church of Christ." It contains numerous essays and articles, histories of churches that have transitioned to an unrestricted practice of assembly leadership, congregational statements on gender equality, and an annotated bibliography. See also Jarrod Robinson, "Owning Up to Our Baptismal Vows" (Galatians 3:26–28), a lecture given at the 2014 Pepperdine Bible Lectures, Malibu, CA, at http://new.livestream.com/pepperdineuniversity/pbl14/videos/49670060. For a more restricted perspective the reader is again referred to Everett Ferguson's *The Church of Christ: A Biblical Ecclesiology for Today* (Eerdmans, 1997), 337–344.

Chapter 5
Will God Forgive Christians Who Fall Away?

A scholarly but accessible article by I. Howard Marshall introduces readers to the doctrines of apostasy, perseverance, and eternal security (http://evangelicalarminians.org/wp-content/uploads/2013/03/Marshall.-The-Problem-of-Apostasy.pdf). A brief response to this essay can be found at http://evangelicalarminians.org/friday-files-marshall-the-problem-of-apostasy-in-new-testament-theology/. In contrast to Marshall, Sam A. Smith argues that salvation is permanent. He says, "a saved person cannot lose their salvation, and . . . it should be clear that those who apostatize were never saved." See the full essay at http://www.biblicalreader.com/btr/Apostasy.htm. Robert Shank wrote two volumes widely read and praised for their exposition of the biblical texts relating to apostasy and security: *Life in the Son: A Study in the Doctrine of Perseverance* (Springfield, MO: Westcott Publishers, 1961) and *Elect in the Son: A Study of the Doctrine of Election* (Springfield, MO: Westcott Publishers, 1970).

Four differing positions on this question are presented in J. Matthew Pinson's *Four Views on Eternal Security* (Grand Rapids, MI: Zondervan, 2002). The four are: Classical Calvinism, Moderate Calvinism, Reformed Arminianism, and Wesleyan Arminianism. The format features an explanation by a representative of that position followed by challenges from advocates of the other positions.

My thought on the interpretation of Hebrews in general and of Hebrews 6:4–6 in particular has been shaped by James W. Thompson's commentary, *Hebrews,* Paideia Commentaries on the New Testament (Grand Rapids, MI: Baker, 2008). In particular, pages 122–124 and 133–135 are enlightening on 6:4–6, and pages 10–28 offer insights regarding the literary nature and philosophical background of the book.

Chapter 6
What Is the Eternal Destiny of Those Who Have Never Heard of Jesus?

What About Those Who Have Never Heard? Three Views on the Destiny of the Unevangelized (Downers Grove, IL: InterVarsity Press, 1995) explores Inclusivism, Postmortem Conversion, and Restrictivism. Sanders, who also edited the volume, argues for Inclusivism. Gabriel Fackre makes the case for Postmortem Conversion. Ronald Nash contends for Restrictivism. Inclusivism is the view that salvation is only through Christ and that people are saved on the basis of believing the revelation that they have. Postmortem Conversion is the view that unevangelized people will get an opportunity to hear the gospel after death. Restrictivism is the view that no one can come to God except through Jesus Christ. Each proponent presents his view and the others respond with critique, so the format itself is a nice model for the kind of forthright but respectful dialogue I advocate here.

Some recent books are re-visiting the doctrine of hell. Among these a few suggest that hell doesn't exist and/or that a loving God could never condemn anyone to an eternity of torment. In *Love Wins: A Book About Heaven, Hell, and the Fate of Every Person Who Ever Lived* (San Francisco: HarperOne, 2012) Rob Bell questions the existence of hell and the traditional view that only those who believe in Jesus will go to heaven. William Crockett, John F. Walvoord, Zachary J. Hayes, and Clark H. Pinnock collaborated to write *Four Views on Hell* (Grand Rapids: Zondervan, 1996). They name these four perspectives Literal, Metaphorical, Purgatorial, and Conditional. In *Surprised by Hope: Rethinking Heaven, the Resurrection, and the Mission of the Church* (New York: HarperCollins, 2008), N. T. Wright argues that the Bible actually says less about hell than evangelical Christians think it does, and that bodily resurrection is what Christians can anticipate. C. S.

Lewis wrote on the question of the after-life in *The Great Divorce* (originally published 1946; San Francisco: HarperOne, 2001).

For more on the view of the unevangelized popularly known as "anonymous Christians" (i.e., the idea, introduced by Catholic theologian Karl Rahner, that non-Christians may be saved through Jesus), see Stephen M. Clinton, *Peter, Paul and the Anonymous Christian: A Response to the Mission Theology of Rahner and Vatican II* (A paper presented to The Orlando Institute Leadership Forum, October 1998). Available at http://www.toi.edu/Resources/Anonomous2.pdf.

To better appreciate the number of the world's unevangelized, see "Key findings of 'Global Christianity: A Report on the Size and Distribution of the World's Christian Population,'" a study by the Pew Research Center's Forum on Religion & Public Life. http://www.pewforum.org/2011/12/19/global-christianity-exec/.

Chapter 7
Is the Lord's Supper a Table or an Altar?

John Mark Hicks argues persuasively for a table view of the Lord's supper in *Enter the Water, Come to the Table* (Abilene, TX: ACU Press, 2014), which contains some new and updated material from his earlier book *Come to the Table: Revisioning the Lord's Supper* (Abilene, TX: Leafwood Publishers, 2002). I have benefitted from Parker J. Palmer's essay, "On Staying at the Table: A Spirituality of Community," and his suggestion that a table is the most appropriate biblical symbol for community. Unfortunately, there does not seem to be a copy of Palmer's essay published in a journal. You can, however, find it reproduced in this blog: http://love2justice.wordpress.com/2011/09/01/the-garden-the-city-and-the-table/. Everett Ferguson provides a thorough biblical introduction to the Lord's supper in *The Church of Christ: An Ecclesiology for Today* (Grand Rapids, MI: Eerdmans, 1996), 249–261.

Chapter 8
Do We Worship on Sunday or Every Day?

Doug Sherman's and William Hendricks's book, *Your Work Matters to God* (Colorado Springs, CO: NavPress, 1987) and William E. Diehl's, *The Monday Connection: On Being an Authentic Christian in a Weekday World* (New York: HarperCollins, 1993) provide practical examinations of daily life as worship.

In *Streams of Living Water: Celebrating the Great Traditions of Christian Faith* (New York: HarperCollins, 1998), Richard Foster explores six traditions (or "streams") Christians have pursued as expressions of their faith and as ways of encountering God. These six traditions are Contemplative (Prayer), Holiness (Virtue), Charismatic (Spirit-empowered), Social Justice (Compassion), Evangelical (Word-centered), and Incarnational (Sacramental). The section on the Incarnational tradition most directly addresses daily life as worship, but this entire book is a great resource for enhancing one's understanding and practice of the spiritual life. Gary L. Thomas does something similar by identifying nine "sacred pathways" through which we connect to God in *Sacred Pathways: Discover Your Soul's Path to God* (Nashville, TN: Thomas Nelson, 1996).

Readers from the heritage of Churches of Christ will resonate (and disagree) with something of the contents of this anonymous blogger: http://freeinchrist.wordpress.com/tag/five-acts-of-worship/. See also, Mike Root, *Spilt Grape Juice: Rethinking the Worship Tradition* (Joplin, MO: College Press, 1992).

CPSIA information can be obtained at www.ICGtesting.com
Printed in the USA
LVOW05s1120250914

405809LV00002B/2/P